Mindset In Motion

Activate Purpose, Power, and Peak Performance

Introducing the 5-Step
Mindset In Motion Method™
By Debbi DiMaggio

Published By
DiMaggio Publishing House

"Look for the extraordinary in the ordinary; that's where the magic lies."

—Debbi DiMaggio

Mindset In Motion™

Published by DiMaggio House Publishing

Activate Purpose, Power, and Peak Performance

Introducing the 5-Step Mindset in Motion Method™

By Debbi DiMaggio

© Debbi DiMaggio March 2026

Debbi DiMaggio

Published by *DiMaggio House Publishing*

Oakland, CA 94618

DebbiDiMaggio.com

Paperback: 979-8-9951152-0-5

ebook: ASIN

Hardcover: 979-8-9951152-1-2

Bestselling Author, Podcast Host, Speaker, Real Estate Advisor

DebbiDiMaggio.com

Endorsements

Debbi DiMaggio's Mindset in Motion is an inspiring, action-driven guide that empowers you to shift your thinking, elevate your habits, and step into your next chapter with confidence. Her proven method is both motivating and practical, perfect for anyone ready to stop playing small and start living with purpose. **—Terry Healey, author of The Resilience Mindset and At Face Value**

Mindset In Motion™ captures something I've seen repeatedly in business and in life: success rarely comes from talent alone – it comes from clarity of purpose followed by disciplined action. This is a thoughtful guide for anyone ready to move from intention to impact. **— Pamela Liebman, President & CEO, The Corcoran Group**

Mindset in Motion delivers a powerful and practical framework for turning vision into action. Debbi DiMaggio combines real-world experience, resilience, and heart to help individuals and teams move beyond self-doubt and create lasting momentum. Her ability to inspire confidence, elevate leadership, and foster meaningful collaboration makes this book a valuable guide for anyone committed to growth and impact. **—Robert Reffkin, CEO, Compass**

Mindset in Motion reminds us that the greatest arena we will ever compete in is the one within. True resilience is a balanced tension between exhaustion and purpose. This book teaches that identity must be defined before victory can be experienced, and that aligned thought becomes aligned action. It is a guide for those ready to lead themselves first, so they may lead others with strength and harmony. **—Flavio Moy, CRP, Transpersonal Therapist, Initiated Shaman**

This can be the year everything shifts—when intention meets momentum. In Mindset in Motion, Debbi reveals a practical, proven system for turning intention into lasting, meaningful results. **—Debi Hemmeter, President Inner Mountain Foundation, Co-Founder Lean In**

Elite performance, whether in business, leadership, or life, starts with clarity and is sustained by disciplined action. In Mindset in Motion, Debbi DiMaggio delivers a practical, results-driven framework that transforms intention into measurable momentum. Her 5-Step Method is not a motivational theory; it is a structured system built from decades of real-world execution. This book is for anyone ready to move beyond hesitation and operate at a higher level." **—Chad Rogers, Original Million Dollar Listing Beverly Hills and LA's Top Realtors**

Debbi DiMaggio's Mindset in Motion resonated with me as a former media executive who now coaches professionals to overcome fear and show up confidently on camera. Debbi shows that real growth comes when we honestly confront what's holding us back and take action. Debbi is a true "doer" and writes with the warmth of a supportive friend while filling the book with practical exercises that prove small steps lead to big outcomes. It feels like encouragement with a game plan. **—Kim Rittberg, 6x Award-Winning Video Coach, Former Media Executive, 2x TEDx Speaker**

Debbi DiMaggio is the master of the 180° turn around. Mindset In Motion™ is a brilliant guide for those ready to stop circling their goals and start moving toward a life of purposeful action.**— Shawn Kunkler, Author, Homeward Associates Founder, & Host of Realtor180**

Debbi DiMaggio beautifully captures what so many people need to hear: it's never too late to step back into the arena. Her five-step framework bridges belief and action in a way that feels both practical and deeply empowering. As someone who understands what it means to pause, rebuild, and re-enter stronger than before, I know how powerful this message truly is. Debbi doesn't just inspire - she activates. She gets things done. *Mindset In Motion*™ will help anyone ready to turn the page and move forward with clarity, confidence, and purpose. **—Elizabeth Andrew, Former Tech CEO | TEDx Speaker | Creator of The 4x4 Method**

On January 2, 2008, I launched Win Realty Advisors—a niche brokerage focused on small investors—right at the start of the Great Recession. People thought I had lost my mind. The economy was collapsing. The naysayers were loud. But I believed. I didn't just hope—it would work. I knew it would. And it did. We became the fastest-growing brokerage in Pennsylvania three years in a row. That success didn't happen by accident. It happened because I followed principles that stand the test of time: collaboration over competition, niche focus, creativity, consistency, communication, and genuine care.

That's why Debbi DiMaggio's The Mindset in Motion Method™ resonates so deeply with me. Her message—Goal. Believe. Internalize. Share. Activate. —perfectly reflects the mindset that drives real, sustainable success. This book affirms what I knew nearly two decades ago: when you combine unwavering belief with aligned action, extraordinary results follow.

Debbi doesn't just talk about mindset—she lives it. She bridges inspiration with execution in a way that is authentic, generous, and powerful. I LOVE this book—and you will too. Thank you, Debbi D—my sister from another mister. **—Gary Wilson, CEO, Global Investor Agent Team**

Dedication

This book is dedicated to the people who believed in possibility when the world felt uncertain. To my husband of 35 years, **Adam Betta**, my partner in life and in business. Thank you for your unwavering support, your courage, and your willingness to take risks alongside me.

To **Heidi Marchesotti**, my long-time business and financial partner, whose strength, clarity, and fearless honesty helped shape the company we built together, to **Mindy Sun**, and to every member of our team who walked this journey with us. And to our families, who supported us through long days, uncertain seasons, and bold decisions, this journey belongs to you as much as it does to us.

To the shining stars of my life, my children, **Bianca** and **Chase**. To **Bianca**, the inspiration and catalyst for my first book, *Contained Beauty, Photographs, Reflections, and Swimming Pools,* and to her younger brother, **Chase**, who ignited the spark behind *Mindset In Motion*™.

For my grandmother, Stella, who always told my father, her son, **Vince DiMaggio**, that I would go on to do great things. She believed in me before I fully believed in myself. My father often repeats her words as I continue to pursue new dreams and create new chapters. She remains my guiding light. In her honor, a portion of the proceeds from this book will be donated to breast cancer causes.

And to my mother, **Midge DiMaggio**, your love, strength, and unwavering support through every chapter of my life mean more than words can express. Thank you for your unwavering support, your courage, and your willingness to sit beside me during the difficult times.

To my family, whose belief in discipline, resilience, and possibility shaped who I am. Someone once asked me a question I'll never forget: "Is it DNA… or Debbi?" Maybe a little of both. As a relative of baseball legend **Joe DiMaggio**, I grew up hearing stories of perseverance, grace, and relentless excellence. His legendary 56-game hitting streak during the 1941 Major League Baseball season proved that greatness is built through discipline and consistency. But what I've learned through life, business, and running the Los Angeles Marathon is this:

Greatness isn't inherited.

It's activated.

This book is for anyone ready to move their mindset into motion and discover what they are truly capable of.

Table Of Content

Mindset in Motion

Foreword

It's fair to say that I knew the name Debbi DiMaggio as I saw her posts appear on various social media platforms. We seemed to know so many of the same people, not necessarily from our professional lives, but from our personal lives in the distant past.

As it turns out, Debbi and I grew up not too far apart, but we both ended up at UC Berkeley, where she literally lived in the house behind mine for several years. How was it that we never bumped into one another at a party, on the street, in the library, or were introduced by one of our mutual friends? It turns out we graduated together in a beautiful ceremony at the Greek Theatre in Berkeley. How was it that we didn't meet in one of our classes? Perhaps it was because I wasn't nearly as diligent as Debbi about attending class.

Fast forward almost forty years. With the launch of my most recent book, *The Resilience Mindset* (9/9/2025), a mutual friend suggested we connect, especially since Debbi hosted a podcast that she thought I would be an appropriate guest for. Turns out we have a lot of common philosophies about mindset and moving forward when confronted with adversity.

What drew me to Debbi's work was her Mindset in Motion Method, which provides a framework to guide readers from intention to execution. So many of us struggle with adapting to change, and not just setting new goals, but achieving them. Debbi's approach provides a practical guide to do just that.

Debbi writes about "the spark" that opens our eyes to what is possible. It's so important to understand this concept. I refer in my own framework to the spark as the turning point and inspiration that comes from daily reflection. These "sparks" are nuggets we must act on, or we'll lose them. We must be comfortable with taking a risk when our gut tells us to. Her concept of 'acting' on that with the end in mind correlates with the power of positive imaging and visualization, a practice that's been part of my daily regimen ever since I faced a life-threatening adversity of my own.

Preparation, getting focused, and setting goals. That's how Debbi's book can help you. Achieving goals (as small as they might be) helps you believe in yourself. This is the stepping stone to building confidence and taking your life to new heights.

Debbi's Mindset in Motion Method is actionable. She provides practical exercises throughout to help you on your journey to reaching your next level, whether that's finding peace with change or getting ahead in business. And sometimes this process requires you to evaluate your relationships and focus on those that provide a positive influence, while removing yourself from negativity.

My favorite story in Debbi's book is the one about her running the LA Marathon, predominantly based on discipline, mindset, and willpower – and not so much on physical training. It's a great story about the power of visualization, and it's what success is predicated on – determination, persistence, and grit.

I love her references to 'halftimes' – moments where we reset, reflect, and figure out how to regroup and refocus. I must say that these 'halftimes' and reflection time led me to my greatest turning points. Pain became a possibility.

Read on and be reminded of one of my most important life philosophies – embrace change, and you will gain tremendous wisdom – and that's a growth mindset in action. **—Terry Healey, Author, *The Resilience Mindset and At Face Value***

Preface

I Ran the LA Marathon on Mindset Alone

My Story

I did not train for the LA Marathon the way most people would define training. I didn't train my body; I trained my mind. And it changed everything. I ran the LA Marathon on mindset alone before my 60th birthday. I had no intention of doing so until 5 words my son said to us while on holiday in St. Barth, enjoying lunch by the beach. But those 5 words he said struck a chord in me so deep. Now, let me be clear, I am not recommending this strategy for your next athletic event. But what I *am* recommending is this: **Mental toughness changes everything.**

People ask me all the time, *"Weren't you scared? Didn't you think it was impossible?"* No. Because before I ever ran a mile, I trained my mind. I immersed myself in the mindset of a soldier and made an unshakable decision. I wasn't fearful. I wasn't hesitant. I didn't question whether I should do it. Once I committed, I committed fully. Waiting for "perfect conditions" has never been part of how I operate. I believe in forward motion, discipline, and showing up, especially when something matters. My mindset training didn't come from running manuals or fitness apps. It came from an intense two-month immersion in the mindset of military heroes and soldiers, men and women who operate under pressure, push through pain, and complete the mission no matter the conditions. It is truly remarkable. Running a marathon is a sliver in comparison.

It also came from reading *You Can't Hurt Me* by **David Goggins.** If **David Goggins** could rise from an unimaginably difficult background and become a Navy SEAL, one of the toughest, most elite achievements in the world, then I knew without question that I could run a marathon. That comparison wasn't arrogance. It was perspective. Hard is relative.

Soldiers are not born; **they are created.** I'm not talking about physical strength. I'm talking about mental discipline. The decision to move forward when your body says stop. The commitment to finishing what you start. Running a marathon was not putting me in harm's way. I wasn't facing injury or death. I wasn't stepping onto a battlefield. I wasn't going to watch people die or live in fear of stepping on a landmine. I was simply running a long, uncomfortable, very boring race. But I had to do it. I needed to know what it felt like to push past my own excuses. And the reason traces back to a conversation with my son. That afternoon, I could see so clearly when he told us he was signing up for OCS, Officer Candidate School, one of the most rigorous military leadership programs in the country. It prepares candidates mentally and physically for extreme responsibility, discipline, and leadership under pressure. I asked him, "Why? We've never talked about this before." He looked at me and said very calmly: **"I want to challenge myself."** And that was all he said.

Mindset in Motion

We went back to playing dominoes, sipping rose, and eating lunch while a group of waiters gathered around our table to watch us play. What struck me, as it were, was that a photographer came over and snapped some shots while I was processing one of the scariest moments in my life. I raised my cheeks to emulate a smile while my head was spinning. I know for a fact that my husband and Chase's sister, Bianca, were as well. I tried to hold back the tears. The crazy thing is that I am always trying to arrange a family photo shoot, and I did not arrange this one, and what precise timing that the photographer came over at this exact moment. A historic and pivotal moment in our lives.

We returned from our trip in mid-December. On December 31st, 2023, I took my first run contemplating Chase's words. Still not quite grasping what he was saying. And as for my decision to run the marathon. There was no drama or grand explanation. Actually, I told no one. The LA Marathon was on March 23rd. I committed in late February, less than one month later. Physically prepared? No. **Mentally prepared? Absolutely.** And here's what I learned: **Your mind will quit 1,000 times before your body ever needs to.** The real marathon isn't the race. It's the conversation you have with yourself. The voice that says

You're too old. You can't do this. You're not fit enough. You haven't trained. Who do you think you are? That is when Mindset answers back: **Watch me.** That marathon wasn't about running. It was about proving to myself that

I could do hard things, on purpose, because I had made up my mind. And you can too. In your life. In your business. In your relationships. In your next chapter. Mindset isn't motivation. It's persistence. It's dedication. It's hard work. And it's surrounding yourself with people who expect you to rise.

On race morning, surrounded by thousands of runners who looked physically prepared, I felt calm and focused. My body knew what it hadn't done, but my mind knew exactly what it *could* do. I had trained it to stay present, to stay committed, and to keep moving forward no matter what showed up. Because mindset isn't about pretending something is easy. It's about refusing to quit when it gets uncomfortable.

As the race began, I broke the marathon into moments instead of miles. I didn't think about 26.2 miles. I focused on the next step. The next breath. The next block. This is straight from military thinking: don't overwhelm the mission; execute the next move. I visualized every part of the race. I knew the streets, from Dodger Stadium to Silver Lake, all the way down Sunset, where I asked my husband to meet me, on the corner of Sunset Blvd. and La Cienega. And on down Doheny to Burton. I was on Burton Way, where things got interesting.

At mile 10, my body checked in. I was fine. By mile 13, my husband shared with our kids and our friends who were tracking my race on their phones, sitting in comfortable chairs, perhaps sipping a cocktail or exerting a little less energy than I. And then at mile 18, it pushed back. At mile 20, it tested me. But there was no way I was going to stop unless I was injured.

And that's where mindset separates people. I didn't negotiate with discomfort. I expected it. Soldiers don't wait to feel good to move forward. They move forward because the mission demands it. I reminded myself that discomfort is temporary, but quitting creates permanence. This wasn't about running. It was about proving that mental discipline outlasts physical readiness. I repeated and convinced myself around mile 17 or 18 that I was fortunate to be physically able to run. So I ran for those who could not run. I relied on structure, self-talk, and discipline, not motivation. Motivation is emotional. Discipline is reliable. I repeated the same truths with every step:

You finish what you start. You stay in control when things get hard. Your mind leads, your body follows.

Oh, and that stubborn mule mindset in me simply would not allow it. Crossing the finish line wasn't just about completing a marathon. It was about confirmation. Proof that when you condition your mind through discipline, exposure to greatness, and belief, you can do extraordinary things without perfect preparation. That day reshaped how I approach everything.

- Business.
- Motherhood.

- Leadership.

- A Cancer Diagnosis.

- Life Transitions.

I stopped asking, "Am I physically ready?" And started asking, "Am I mentally committed?" And yes, I can do whatever I need to accomplish my goals. Because commitment changes outcomes. Discipline creates momentum. And mindset determines how far you go.

The LA Marathon reinforced what I already knew to be true:

You don't need ideal circumstances to begin your next chapter. You need clarity. You need to resolve. And you need the courage to execute, one step at a time. If others can overcome the impossible through mental toughness, then so can you. Your limits are far beyond what you think, once your mind is trained to lead and say YES!

That's what *Mindset in Motion* is about. Because the moment you decide to challenge yourself, everything changes. And sometimes the finish line you're chasing isn't 26.2 miles away. **It's one decision away.**

The Extraordinary in the Ordinary

In 2008, during one of the most uncertain economic seasons of our lifetime, many people were stepping back. We chose to step forward. We did not have the perfect plan, polished branding, or all the answers. What we had was grounded belief, hard work, and a deep desire to serve others with authenticity and heart.

Looking back, I now see that extraordinary companies such as Airbnb, Uber, and Square were also born during that same challenging time. Their stories remind us that innovation and courage often grow in moments of uncertainty. At the time, we were simply responding to what was in front of us. We kept moving forward.

One afternoon, not long after we started, my husband Adam, our business partner Heidi, and I were driving to a listing presentation. It was a beautiful home overlooking the entire San Francisco Bay. The sellers were interviewing multiple agents, and the stakes felt high.

The night before, I had stayed up late creating a CMA, our little black book, filled with charts, statistics, company information, and everything I thought we needed to prove ourselves. I wanted it to be perfect.

As we approached the home, Adam sat in the front seat while I handed the black book to Heidi in the passenger seat. She began flipping through the pages.

Rip. "We don't need this."

Rip. "We don't need that."

Rip. "This isn't who we are."

Papers flew everywhere. In the car, on the floor, in the air. My heart was racing. By the time we pulled into the driveway, the CMA I spent so much time creating remained in shreds on the floor of the car. Heidi turned to us and said, "We don't need any stinking books. It's about us. It's about what we can do for them."

At that moment, something shifted. We walked into that home with nothing in our hands except confidence, authenticity, and the belief that we could help. We listened. We connected. And we got the listing. That day, I learned one of the greatest lessons of my career: It is not about the company. It is not about the presentation. It is not about perfection. It is about people. It is about connection. It is about showing up as your true self and trusting that your intention and experience will guide the way.

Years later, when my son reminded me of that moment and how we launched HIGHLAND PARTNERS, he said, "Mom, you guys started a company in a recession." I realized something powerful. We didn't always know. We simply kept moving forward. Over time, this became the foundation of what I now call the **Mindset In Motion Method™**.

It is not complicated. It is a way of living. A belief that clarity comes from action, and confidence is built through movement.

Through my work in real estate, coaching, my podcast, *Mastering the Art of Success, and in life,* I have seen this truth unfold again and again. Families navigating change. Entrepreneurs building new futures, and rising up again after a fall. Individuals rediscovering purpose in seasons they never expected. This book is an invitation. An invitation to trust yourself. An invitation to embrace change. An invitation to take action before you feel completely ready.

Most of all, it is an invitation to look for the extraordinary in the ordinary, because that is where the magic lies. Whether you are beginning something new, navigating uncertainty, or simply feeling called to grow, my hope is that these pages will remind you that you already have what you need. You only need to begin.

With gratitude,

Debbi DiMaggio

Introduction

"Movement itself generates momentum, excitement, and purpose."

The Science of Action, The Art of Becoming When we talk about goals, most people focus on the finish line, on the achievement, the outcome, the accomplishment itself. But the truth, both scientifically and spiritually, is far more profound. Happiness doesn't come *after* you achieve your goals. Fulfillment doesn't appear *once* everything is complete. Confidence isn't something you earn at the end.

It's Created In The Doing

Every step you take toward a meaningful goal, no matter how small, activates real shifts within you. Dopamine fuels excitement. Serotonin steadies your spirit. Flow state sharpens your focus. And with each action, your self-efficacy grows: "I can do this." I am capable. I am becoming." Movement becomes momentum. Momentum becomes confidence. Confidence becomes identity.

Science confirms what you already know: You feel better when you are in motion. Not because motion guarantees success, but because motion makes you feel alive, aligned, and in command of your life.

This is the essence of Mindset in Motion. It's not about perfection, speed, or certainty. It's about choosing purposeful movement, one aligned step at a time, and allowing your mindset and intention to carry you forward. Your next chapter doesn't begin when the goal is achieved. It begins the moment you decide to take action. The moment you begin, you change. The moment you take action, you rise. The moment you move toward your dreams, your life expands.

The Spark, Be Open to the Possibilities

"One conversation can change everything. One spark can ignite a whole new chapter in your life."

<u>The Whirlpool Spark</u>

It started with a conversation. Or rather, it started with a decision to speak and get out of my comfort zone. I was sitting in the whirlpool at Voda Spa, a private social club in Los Angeles. I'd been alternating between the hot sauna and cold plunge, one of my favorite rituals. If you've ever done this circuit, you know it breaks down walls, mentally and physically. You surrender to the shock, the sweat, and the clarity it brings.

Three men were rotating through the circuit alongside me. We kept bumping into one another, sharing that silent acknowledgment you give to familiar strangers. Eventually, we ended up in the whirlpool at the same time. And as you will learn in this book, it is mindset, momentum, and a strong belief that new doors and opportunities are opened through action. So, I introduced myself. It started with a decision to speak and step out of my comfort zone.

"Hi, I'm Debbi. What's your name?" They each shared theirs, Alexander among them. And what followed was not small talk but a much deeper and more interesting conversation than I had expected. Alexander told me he owned a treatment center. I asked what kind. He replied, "Have you heard of AA?" Everyone has. "Not in our culture," he said. "In Armenian families, it's taboo. We're not taught about it. Addiction isn't discussed. Weakness is shameful. In our culture, a man is supposed to handle "it" on his own."

I was stunned. I was sitting in the whirlpool with very buff, tattooed, confident men. The kind of men you might assume ran nightclubs, boxed professionally, or, if I'm being honest, were part of the Mafia or the Cartel. But here they were quite the opposite, emotionally intelligent, self-aware, gentle, kind, and passionate about helping others break the cycle of addiction in a culture that didn't give them tools to do so.

One had been sober for eight years. Another three. They told me about the outings they took their recovery group on, holiday vacations, workouts, and team-building exercises. They had created a brotherhood around healing. And they were not ashamed or weak. What struck me most was how open they were. And how ready they were to break generational cycles and redefine masculinity and strength.

In that moment, I shared what I did, not just that I work in real estate, but that I write, coach, and had recently developed a method based on how I've achieved my own goals over a lifetime. I explained how it all started and the concept of 'reverse engineering.' I mentioned running the LA Marathon without proper training, publishing multiple books, launching a podcast, overcoming the empty nest, building a successful real estate business, launching a new real estate company during a recession, and helping others break through barriers to start new chapters of their own.

You never know what might come out of a conversation.

"I believe there is always a spark waiting to be discovered when you are open to the possibilities."

And the next morning, I experienced that spark. It's a spark I've come to love and enjoy, one that revs my engine. The wheels begin to turn, my mind starts firing ideas, and eventually, I am compelled to get up and write.

I realized the same strategy I used to run the LA Marathon, write books, build a business, and launch my podcast could be used to beat addiction. It starts with five intentional steps I call **The Mindset In Motion Method**™. I arrived at this method by reverse-engineering how I had achieved my goals over the years. And that became the foundation of The Mindset In Motion Method™. The method is universal. Whether you're training your body, losing unwanted pounds, launching a business, seeking to double or triple your income, healing your heart, or freeing yourself from addiction, transformation always begins the same way, with a crystal clear goal, direction and intention.

The Mindset In Motion Method™

1. **GOAL**: Set the goal: sobriety, wellness, achievement.

2. **BELIEVE**: Replace the negative loop "I can't" with "I will."

3. **INTERNALIZE:** Visualize it, sit with it, embrace it, and embody it.

4. **SHARE:** Verbalize it. Say it out loud. Let others in. Take Note: Only share it with *supportive people* who want to see you accomplish your goals.

5. **ACTIVATE:** Commit to the work. Show up daily. Stay consistent. Engage the right support. Execute.

Set the five steps into motion, and goals turn into results. that's **the Mindset In Motion Method**™ at work. Mindset is not fluff, it's the foundation of transformation. Elite athletes and top business performers share one thing: discipline, focus, and mental resilience.

The Mindset in Motion Method reveals how world-class competitors train their minds, not just their bodies. You can do the same to elevate your business game, or personal life. In this book, you'll learn to:

- Build unstoppable confidence and laser-sharp focus

- Turn pressure into performance and setbacks into comebacks

- Create winning routines, habits, and rituals for success

- Lead with clarity, purpose, and resilience

Blending real-world and personal stories with proven psychological tools, this book is your playbook for dominating your goals in business, leadership, and life.

<u>Why Mindset in Motion</u>

Movement Is Medicine, and It will change your life. What if I hadn't spoken up in that whirlpool? What if I'd stayed in my head and not opened that conversation? I would not have learned something new. A new idea would not have ignited. And I would not be writing this section of this book.

Everything begins with a choice to move, from silence to speech, from doubt to belief, from pause to power.

That's **The Mindset In Motion Method™** in action.

<u>Who This Book Is For</u>

Mindset isn't something you switch on, it's something you train, like a muscle. Transformation doesn't happen by accident. It happens by intention. This book is for anyone with a goal, a passion, a dream, or an obstacle to overcome.

Your goal may be health related, career growth, overcoming an addiction, navigating the empty nest, healing from divorce, or launching a business. The possibilities are endless. If you're unsure where to start, ask yourself: What am I avoiding? What makes my heart race when I think about it? That's your starting point.

When we are working towards conquering our goals and finding success, oftentimes we look to our role models and mentors, even athletes. Athletes often possess unique traits that contribute to their success as founders, CEOs, or entrepreneurs. You may not know, I am related to Joe DiMaggio, but I am not an all-time hero athlete like Joe. I have dabbled, that's for certain, but I'm not a professional athlete. I do, however, think like one, and that is why this book is structured like a sports game. Whether it's football or basketball, pickle ball or tennis, competitive swimming or track, this book is outlined from the point of view of a game. Choose your favorite sport and follow along. From Pre-Game preparation, Game Execution, and Post-Game reflection. Whatever sport you are passionate about, you know the rhythm. Prepare. Perform. Reflect. That's the rhythm of this book. That's the rhythm of transformation.

Why This Book Exists

My goal is to help you succeed. This book is for anyone at a turning point, whether you're starting something new, recovering from a breakup, navigating unchartered waters, dealing with burnout, or simply ready to take action. You don't need to have it all figured out. You need a method that works. And the courage to start.

How To Read This Book

When I read, or listen to an audiobook, podcast, or vlog, I am usually compelled to stop and take notes as I am often inspired to put something into motion long before I am done with the lesson. I want this book to be one that you will refer to time and time again. A pocketbook you can open up to any page to find inspiration and guidance. You can read this book straight through, or flip to any section that speaks to where you are in your life, at that moment.

At the end of each chapter, you'll find space to write notes. Use it. The insights that matter most to you are worth capturing. If you are so inspired, you might have a journal, or use the Notes feature on your mobile device, or open up your laptop and start a new Google Doc so you can write out all of your thoughts and ideas.

So grab your favorite pen and a highlighter and mark the moments that move you, the brilliant nuggets of insight and inspiration you'll want to return to again and again. At the end of each chapter, you'll engage with three prompts:

GOAL: What are you working toward?

ACTION: Small steps to move you forward. What's one small step you can take today?

CONNECT: List the names of friends, clients, colleagues, acquaintances, and even new connections you can reach out to for encouragement, insight, collaboration, or opportunities that will help you move forward with your goals.

This is not just a book, it's your playbook.
Your blueprint for success.

Its purpose is simple – to ignite a spark within, and propel you forward.

What Is Mindset

[Mindset] noun. The driving force in the quest for success and achievement. A mindset that combines discipline, strength, confidence, and ambition is a powerful mindset. This can achieve anything it sets its sights on. A powerful mind can achieve anything.

What Is Motion?

The action or process of moving or being moved.

"Always be moving forward. Don't look back, you're not going that way."

When I look at an athlete, I see someone focused, determined, and committed to the work no matter what it takes. CEOs and business leaders embrace these same qualities. They train their minds as rigorously as athletes train their bodies. You don't need to be an athlete to think like one. You need curiosity about what makes top performers unstoppable, and the willingness to apply those same principles to your own goals.

Transitioning To Win

Life is made up of transitions, some you choose, some that choose you. These moments hold the key to growth. Through mindset shifts and accountability, I've learned that success isn't just possible. It's inevitable when you have the right framework. In this book, I'll share the story of how I discovered this method, the practical steps to implement it, and how it will help you navigate your own transition, whatever that looks like for you. Business is the ultimate sport.

If you want to lead, grow, and perform at the highest level, you need more than talent. You need grit, strategy, and the mindset of a champion. This book is your playbook for high performance.

You'll learn to:

- Turn pressure into fuel and bounce back
- Train your mind for focus, confidence, and clarity
- Build unstoppable habits and championship-level discipline
- Lead with precision and passion

No fluff. No hype. Just battle-tested strategies.

<u>Game On</u>

Life is made up of transitions. Some you choose, some choose you. In either case, you decide how you respond.

You do not need permission.

You don't need perfect conditions.

You need a system.

You need momentum.

You need the courage to begin.

Your next chapter starts today. Let's go.

PART 1
Pre-Game

Chapter 1

Pre-Game Mindset

"No matter how you feel, get up, dress up, show up, and never give up."

I ran the Los Angeles Marathon on mindset alone. No training. No preparation. Just belief. At the time, my son was preparing for OCS, Officer Candidate School, to become a Marine. When I asked him why, he simply said, "I want to challenge myself." That single statement ignited a fire within me unlike anything I had ever felt before.

I became fascinated with the military mindset. I watched YouTube video after video, immersed myself in military preparedness, and listened to podcasts and books on Audible, anything I could get my hands on. Among them was a life-changing book by David Goggins, CAN'T HURT ME, where he recounts his extraordinary journey from a childhood marked by poverty, abuse, and neglect to overcoming obesity and running on broken shins, ultimately transforming himself into a Navy SEAL and one of the world's toughest endurance athletes.

Everything I consumed made me realize that with the right mindset, anything is possible, which led me to reflect more deeply on what my son meant when he said, "challenge myself."

I decided I would put my own mindset to the test. As soon as New Year's Eve, 2023, turned into New Year's Day, 2024, I signed up for every race I could find, multiple 10Ks, a half-marathon trail run, three Spartan races, even the LA Marathon (after just 2.5 months into my new challenge) the entire 26.2 miles of it! I didn't overthink it. I just dove in. I needed to know what was possible when you rely on MINDSET alone.

People often confuse mindset with "positive thinking." But mindset is so much more than optimism or good vibes. Mindset is how you *live*. It's your internal framework. It's the decision you make, every single day, to keep showing up, no matter what. It's what helps you reboot after a setback. It's the fuel that gets you out of bed when doubt creeps in. And the foundation beneath every action you take.

> **"Action builds momentum. Momentum builds confidence. And confidence delivers results."**

The dictionary defines mindset as "the established set of attitudes held by someone." So, to understand what your mindset is and how to improve it, it's important to look under the hood of what makes you tick.

An **Attitude** is emotional, it's how you feel about a situation. Are you optimistic, cheerful, and hopeful, and choosing to see the good in every situation? Or do you feel overwhelmed and discouraged when you face a setback? Do you think people are mostly good? Or mostly out to get you? Maybe your plans got canceled at the last minute. What's your attitude towards it? Do you sulk, or do you think, *"Perfect! I'll take a breath, reset, and maybe even get ahead on something else."*

Your **Mindset** is the lens through which you see the world, yourself, your potential, and what's possible. It's not fleeting. It doesn't depend on whether you had your matcha or got stuck in traffic. It's your inner compass. **When things go sideways, your mindset determines if you crumble... or recalibrate.** It's what says, "This *isn't the end, it's just a pivot. What's the lesson? What's the next move?"*

During the LA Marathon, around mile 18, when fatigue kicked in, and doubt *tried* to creep in, my inner voice came through loud and clear: **"You are not an 'almost.' You finish what you begin."**

Finishing what I start has been my attitude towards life since I was young. As a result, I knew I would cross the finish line. This is the power of mindset. When you deliberately foster a mindset that helps you succeed, you become unstoppable. Have you ever watched an Olympic swimmer, diver, gymnast, or figure skater and wondered, *how does one become that good?* As a high achiever my entire life and a mother of a high-achieving athlete, I've had a front-row seat to the level of mental discipline and stamina that goes into achieving that level of physical competence. An athlete doesn't just show up to the game. He **prepares.** He **trains his mind** as much as his body.

He develops the resilience to show up even when he doesn't feel like it. That is what I call the **winning mindset.** High-level performers in any field, whether in athletics, business, or personal pursuits, embrace a winning mindset.

Sure, talent can provide a great foundation, but without motivation and consistency, talent can only get you so far. The world is full of very talented people who were not able to achieve the type of success they knew they were capable of achieving because they lacked a winning mindset. A winning mindset means you show up every single day with structure, discipline, and focus, *especially* when you don't feel like it. This allows you to build momentum that turns your talent into excellence.

There are a few key attributes that create the blueprint of the winning mindset: structure, consistency, and follow-through. A person who practices the winning mindset does not allow a setback or a missed opportunity to knock them down. Instead, they remain resilient and laser-focused. Personally, when I am working on a project or goal, I **LOCK IN** and nothing can get in my way. I become so immersed; it's as if I have strapped into an intense amusement park ride, and there is only one direction: straight ahead with blinders on.

Have you ever been so immersed in a book, or task that you don't even hear your name being called? That is what it means to be *Locked In*. What I've observed in high achievers and athletes is that they readily **Lock In** to the task in front of them. They eliminate all distractions and become single-minded about the result they are trying to achieve. The Winning Mindset, at its core, has only two main components: **Locking In and Taking Action**.

<u>Allow A Setback To Fuel Your Dedication</u>

You might know Michael Jordan as one of the greatest basketball players of all time. But did you know that he was cut from his high school basketball team? Instead of giving up, he used this setback to fuel his dedication. He locked in. Becoming a great basketball player became his number one goal. This determination fueled his ability to show up every day, train harder, and push himself beyond what anyone else might have thought was possible. Eventually, he led the Chicago Bulls to six NBA championships.

When you lock in, you become fully committed to your goal, and nothing can derail you. You follow the blueprint, structure, consistency, and follow-through, and you get it done. When you eliminate distractions, it gives you direction. You either succeed, or you learn, and you try again.

Michael Jordan's story is not uncommon among professional athletes. Often, the highest performers face a setback or rejection early in their careers. Then they lock in, and everything else fades away. They become single-minded in their focus, I refer to this as *laser focus*. My husband can tell when I am working on something and am laser-focused. He knows nothing can draw me out when I am concentrating and locked in. During the COVID-19 lockdown, I was catching up with a friend. It had been a while, but with certain people, time doesn't matter, you pick right up where you left off. As we talked about life and what she'd been doing, I asked her about her book. I remembered those early days when our children were very young; we would visit her and her husband and their dogs, who our kids loved to play with. I recall the sheets of double-spaced typed pages taped floor to ceiling across her pristine white walls. That book had lived there for many years.

Fast forward 20 years, and it still wasn't complete. Life, as it does, simply got in the way, family, obligations, and distractions. When I realized she hadn't published it, I told her, "I'm going to coach you through this. No charge. We're going to get this done together." And that's exactly what we did. We locked in and got moving.

With weekly calls and small, clear assignments, we transformed hesitation into progress. Her life hadn't suddenly become easier. Nothing had changed in her environment. But we changed her mindset, and with my help, she became single-minded about her goal. One of the obstacles she had faced was a lack of accountability. So together, we tackled the book with weekly meetings, follow-up texts, and a steady flow of completed tasks. Bit by bit, locking in made it easier for her to follow through.

"When we have a cheerleader, an accomplice, or an accountability partner, what once seemed insurmountable almost becomes easy."

Next, we confronted her internal roadblocks. She didn't want to share the book with her parents. We worked through it. She was afraid to tell her friends the book was finally happening, after all, they'd known for years it was "in progress." We tackled that fear, too.

She didn't know how, nor did she feel comfortable about creating a Facebook group for her supporters. But together, we worked through that resistance, and locking in made that happen, too. And what followed was a published book, a stronger connection with her family, rekindled friendships from college and other tight-knit communities, and multiple book signings. And that was just the beginning.

When you lock in, you become more confident, resilient, and joyful. You stop making excuses, you limit negative self-talk and distractions, and you move from inaction into motion. My friend's sense of self expanded when she made that commitment to herself, and this major personal milestone opened doors she never imagined were waiting.

"When you lock in, you are choosing your dreams over your fears."

<u>Strategies To Lock In</u>

When I run, I wear headphones so I can focus on running. When I work, I do the same. I put on my noise-canceling headphones to cut out distractions. I do the same when I'm on an airplane and need to concentrate, whether I am reading, writing, or just want to think. Cutting out external noises allows me to *lock in.* By eliminating distractions, I am able to settle into a laser-focused zone that helps me focus on the task at hand.

Distractions are the enemy of locking in. Whether it's the distraction of noise or the distraction of other people, if you want to lock in, you will need to cancel the chatter. This means tidy up your workspace, clear your mind regularly with tools like meditation, use noise-canceling headphones, and create space in your schedule to simply be with yourself.

3 Steps to Locking In:

1. Identify the time and location. Will that be at home, in a cafe, at the library, or at another location?

2. If need be, let your roommate, spouse, children, or co-workers know you will be unavailable for a designated time period and cannot be distracted.

3. Set a timer to allow yourself the time to settle in and begin working.

Note: After you are settled, headphones on, and in your desired location, do not allow yourself to pick up your phone, look at your phone, or check your email. Put all distractions away for that designated time you chose, and stick to it.

The second part of the Lock in Method is taking action. Action creates momentum, and it is momentum that propels us forward. When you lock in, things like structure, planning, consistency, and follow-through become natural. You become laser-focused, moving towards your target. A bee might be buzzing around your ear, but when you are locked in, you don't even notice it. A baby crying in the distance may not even register. It is just not a part of your vortex. When you are locked in, you are in your own world. And that is when you are in a flow state.

When I set out to run the LA Marathon, I had no doubt in my mind that I would finish. I could not tell you when I would finish or how I would feel during the race, but I knew I would lock in and keep moving. The only obstacle that would preclude me from finishing that race would be if I tripped and fell, sprained an ankle, or something I had not even considered could occur.

I had been listening to David Goggins' *Can't Hurt Me*, and his story of running on broken shins, overcoming obesity to become a Navy SEAL made me realize I *had it easy*. My legs worked. My heart was strong. My mind was in it. All that was left for me to do was to take action. So I did. That is the power of mindset, when ACTION is paired with the willingness and determination to move forward.

This can be analogized to a rocket locking onto a target. Once it's locked in, it now has direction, but it still needs some kind of combustion to move it toward that target. Once you lock into a goal, your next step is to put energy behind that intention so you can step into action. You must remain focused while pushing energy towards your goal. There is no time to waste, no time to look for excuses; you are locked in and focused on that one thing, the mission and task at hand.

Forward movement puts you into action. It's as simple as that. Don't make excuses, and don't talk yourself out of doing what in your heart you want to do. Leave the negative self-talk behind. You are your own cheerleader, your goals begin and end with you. And within a team, each person in a company or on the sports field must do their part to elevate the team in order to succeed or win.

When my daughter needed help, I was in New York less than 24 hours later. You might say I was on a mission, a mother's mission, one of those most cherished times. I booked a flight, left San Francisco early that morning, and was by her side in time for dinner.

The first thing I told her was simple but powerful: "Just breathe. Pause. Everything is going to be okay." I asked her to think about the worst-case scenario. What did she believe was the absolute worst thing that could happen? I had her imagine it fully so we could walk through it together. Because so often, the fears we play out in our minds are far worse than reality. Begin with, what am I afraid of? That question usually puts things into perspective.

I reminded her: *Even if you leave your job and don't land a new one right away, you have options.* You have us back in California. You have not only a place to live, but a home. You have my pied-à-terre in Los Angeles. And plenty of friends and family. You have a tremendous support system. In other words, *if there's an emergency landing, it'll be a soft one.* Of course, leaving New York wasn't what she wanted. But she needed to know she had a safety net. That knowledge gave her space to breathe, reflect, and reset. Sometimes, when you are going through a difficult time, it's difficult to take action because you're not able to see the way out. Every path forward might feel overwhelming. I liken it to hitting a brick wall with no idea how to move around it.

Before you lock in and take action, it's more effective to pause and reground yourself first. While action will eventually bring clarity, it's difficult to know what action to take when your life and thoughts feel like they are spinning out of control. That is why I asked my daughter to imagine the worst-case scenario. Once you identify your biggest fear, you can reset and start again, this time with a clean slate and a new mindset. Once you've grounded yourself, you'll feel ready to move forward. The Mindset in Motion Method teaches that when in doubt, get into motion.

Once she was able to calm down and reset, she was ready to lock into a clearly defined goal, which was to land a job that would allow her to stay in New York. Next was to break the monumental task into smaller, more digestible steps, so the goal becomes manageable. Once she locked into her goal, a plan of action appeared.

- Hire a resume writer.

- Reorganize her apartment.

- Take a yoga class.

- Meet with a business mentor.

- Converse with a shaman, therapist, or coach.

- Connect with colleagues for support and insight.

Bianca had never called on me in this way before, and honestly, it felt wonderful to be there for her. To be the one she trusted to walk with her through it. It became a moment I'll always treasure. A real turning point, not just for her, but for us.

Sometimes, what you need most isn't a solution but a **sounding board.** Someone who listens. Someone who cares. Someone who reminds you you're not alone. In the end, all I did was show up, guide her, and set her in motion. She did the heavy lifting. Once she was locked in, taking action became easy.

Regardless of what your goal is, having a plan of action in place will allow you to achieve your goal. This is why companies with written business plans grow

30% faster, according to the *Journal of Management Studies*. Businesses with a clear plan are **far more likely to secure funding** than those without. (*University of Oregon Department of Economics*). Both in your personal and professional life, writing down your goals increases your chances of achieving them by **42%**, compared to those who only think about their goals. (*Jake & Gino*)

In order to write down your goal, you have to first lock in and internalize it. That's the level of clarity that you need to materialize your vision. It's no wonder then that **71% of the fast-growing companies** use strategic plans or long-range planning tools. (*Journal of Small Business Management & Bplans*). They define their goals with specificity to lock in, make a plan, and take action.

"If you fail to plan, you are planning to fail."

– Benjamin Franklin

"Planning is intention in motion. Discipline is preparation in action. No one can do the work for you, align your mind and move."

Mindset In Action

I get a bit low when the real estate market slows. I'm someone who thrives on movement, momentum, and always being in action. It was early August, one of those quiet mornings when I woke up, as I often do, sometime around 3:30 AM. The night still lingered, and the stars and moon were still shining. This time of day is magic to me.

It's my favorite hour in the entire 24 hours we are given, quiet, full of possibility, and deeply reflective.

But as usual, in August, that familiar funk crept in. The market had stalled. I had nothing but time to kill and space to worry. Would I ever have another client? Would I ever sell another house again? It's not rational, I know that. But it's a loop that plays in my head every year around this time, and even though I try to prepare for it, it still finds me. So, as I've always done, I pushed forward. I allowed my imagination to guide me. I got online. I searched YouTube. I listened. I leaned in. That year, I locked into Dr. Joe Dispenza, The Secret, and multiple channels focused on daily affirmations. I cannot tell you how many times I listened, and re-played their stories and each narrator. It was also when Mel Robbins came onto my radar, igniting a fire within me. Whether I was lying in bed, walking, running, flying, or on vacation, I had my headphones on, immersed in a steady stream of positive input. I was reprogramming my mind, moment by moment.

One quote stood out and anchored me:

"Courage doesn't always roar. Sometimes courage is the quiet voice at the end of the day saying, 'I will try again tomorrow."

— Mary Anne Radmacher

That line gave me permission to feel what I felt, and keep going. It reminded me that courage isn't always loud. Sometimes, it's soft. It's subtle. It's the gentle nudge that says, "You've got this. One more day. Try, and try again. I wasn't in a great place. But I pushed through anyway. That is a winning mindset. And, just like clockwork, as the slowness of August passed, **life picked up again that September**.

"Success doesn't happen without mental resilience."

Setbacks will come. Frustration will surface. Slow times are inevitable. No matter how hard we try, we will still find ourselves in a funk from time to time. You may even lose your footing. But do not lose sight of your goal. Strengthen your mindset to silence negative self-talk and block out the noise of others' opinions. The only voice that matters is your own. That August, and every August since, I remind myself of my very own advice: If you don't feel like it, **just start**.

If you're overwhelmed, **follow a plan**. If you're stuck, **move your body, and your head** will catch up.

Tools For A Winning Mind

When you are in a funk and want to get moving, do this:

- Write out your goals, daily, on a piece of paper, in your iPhone Notes, or in a Google Doc.
- Lock into the goal. Imagine yourself already there.

- Become aware of **self-talk**, is it pushing you forward or holding you back?

- Ask yourself: *Who do I want to become? What do I need to do?*

- Make a plan, create an action list, and commit to it daily.

- Visualize the outcome. **Brainwash yourself** with positivity.

- Every morning, move your body. Get up. Get dressed. Get out.

"Let the motion shift your mindset."

Discipline and structure are the foundation of any goal. Without discipline, there is no forward movement. Without structure, there's no direction. You can't move forward if you do not know where you're going, or how you will get there.

Start with the end in mind. Solve for X. What's the question? What are you trying to solve? What's your goal? Where do you want to be? When you begin with the end in mind and reverse engineer the path forward, what I call *The Mindset in Motion Method*™, clarity emerges. And with clarity comes strategy, intentional planning, and focused action toward the result you are committed to achieving.

<u>GOALS | Write It Out</u>

- What is one goal I have been putting off because I did not feel ready?

____

____

- What would happen if I stopped waiting and just started?

____

____

<u>Action | Move Forward</u>

- Write down my current mindset: Is it working for me?

____

____

- Write down **3** beliefs that are holding me back.

____

____

<u>CONNECT | Who Can Help Me?</u>

- A mentor, coach, or accountability partner?

____

____

- A friend who believes in me?

____

____

- Share my goal with someone who will support me. Take action. Reach out today.

____

____

Chapter 2

Preparation Is Key

"The only thing that's keeping you from getting what you want is the story you keep telling yourself." —Tony Robbins

When I left home and went off to college, the daily structure of life, as I knew it, dissipated. It was a very traumatic experience. All of a sudden, time was open. I could go to school if I wanted. I didn't have to go to school if I didn't want to. (But I always did.) It was up to me how I would structure my day, as there was no set schedule I had to adhere to. I didn't have to come home after school and didn't have to tell anyone where I was.

I felt out of sorts. My environment felt a bit out of control, even if just in my head. This newfound freedom, I did not really like it. I was brought up with rules, direction, and boundaries. My parents were not too strict, but the ground rules they did have made me feel safe. In college, all of that structure dissipated, and I was on my own, having to make my own decisions, like it or not. I was a rule follower, so I went to school. I even took an 8 AM class, voluntarily. I recall a roommate telling me that I did not have to sign up for 8 AM classes and that I could sign up for classes at or after noon, if I so desired. That just did not compute. In my mind, school began at 8, maybe 8:30 AM.

In my dorm, we only had eight flat mates, two girls per room. It was a small group, and you were noticed if you weren't going along with the crew. Some of the girls simply did not go to school, and most partied all the time. My roommate smoked pot constantly. She was either sitting in the dark or sleeping more than half the time, very bat-like. I could not have been more opposite. I loved light and having everything open. Another girl chose soap operas over going to class. In those first few weeks, I quickly learned, anything was possible, and there were no boundaries. I did not appreciate the fact that college allowed students the freedom to do whatever they desired. To me, my peers were not preparing themselves properly for success. I was lost without my daily routine, to say the least. I tried to create a structure, but it was difficult. And I did seek friendships outside my flat.

When our kids went off to college, it was extremely important to my husband, Adam, and me that we properly prepared them and set them up for success. We discussed the importance of getting involved and being part of a community. We explained how being involved in a community would give them structure, a network of friends, and camaraderie. I suggested to my daughter that she join a sorority so she'd experience a strong network to support her in her new environment. She was resistant at first, but I convinced her to rush and pledge anyway. It only lasted a year.

In the end, her dormmates that freshman year, and throughout her college years, became her best friends.

Because of the incredible community and bonds she and her friends created those first few months, our daughter had a fantastic and fulfilling college experience. She is still best friends with that large, tight-knit community, and those friendships have continued over the years.

When our son attended the same college, the University of Colorado, Boulder, he was already a step ahead of most freshman students, as he had experienced college life the summer prior when his sister made introductions to other students. He was also on the lacrosse team, which provided not only community but also a structured environment with very full days. He, too, came to nurture a great group of friends, which provided him with a well-rounded and happy college experience.

Whether you are in college or a young adulthood in your 20s and beyond, it's up to you to surround yourself with quality individuals. When you don't, what occurs usually isn't productive and can be unhealthy, even dangerous. A poor choice in friends, a single friend or a significant other who does not have a healthy mindset and who might be involved in drugs or heavy drinking, stealing, gambling, playing non-stop video games, or simply staying up all night, can easily steer you off track, even derail you. You cannot do your best the following day if you do not set yourself up for success the day or night before.

The goal of this book, and of this chapter is all about preparation. Preparation is key, and by aligning yourself with quality individuals you will be encouraged to follow suit, and vice versa.

Motivational speaker, Jim Rohn, says that we are the average of the five people we spend the most time with This relates to the law of averages, which is the theory that the result of any given situation will be the average of all outcomes.

If I had hung out with my dormmates that freshman year, I do not think I would have left USD to go on and graduate from the University of California at Berkeley. If I had skipped class and hung out with my roommate watching soaps, how long would it have taken before I realized I needed to move on or fail out of college? I do not recall exactly, but I believe two or more of the eight received D's, and one even failed out that first year. You do have the choice to make a good decision. It's up to you to make the right decision and prepare for your future and what will be next.

How are you going to prepare for that basketball game, that music concert, or that exam? You must prepare. It's the first step toward success. It is a mindset. If your mindset is that you spend your days and nights with the partiers and skip class or work, see how far that'll take you. Or are you going to level up, train your mind, your body, and the people you hang out with, in order to excel and achieve your goals? Small steps made in one's life result in big changes. Yes, it occurs over time, but you must walk before you jog and jog before you sprint.

I didn't follow the herd, as I knew it was not the right environment for me. I am not going to lie, it doesn't feel great, especially as a freshman, to be on the outside. But I had a goal, which was to get to UC Berkeley. I had the guidance and wisdom of a boyfriend and a high school friend who told me what I had to do to get to Cal. I followed their plan to a tee and graduated from UC Berkeley with a degree in political science. My degree did not have anything to do with what I do today as a real estate advisor, or an author, but they were formative years spent learning, having experiences, and simply growing up.

It's no different from a mother or father who takes their child out for the day and doesn't properly prepare. It's not unusual, it happens. We get busy, distracted, and even forgetful. My friend was traveling with her friends in Paris, and her parents forgot to pack extra diapers, water, snacks, and a coloring book or toy to keep her busy. Even an adult will get cranky without food, water, and a charged cell phone! You get the point. Dwight D. Eisenhower said it best,

"Plans are nothing; planning is everything."

If you want to lose weight or get in shape, set yourself up for success. Keep your refrigerator stocked with fruits and vegetables, lean protein, and other healthy options, and free of sugary and processed food and drinks. And do not keep cookies or other unhealthy pre-packaged items in your home either. No excuses; just don't do it if your goal is to slim down.

If your goal is to get fit? Start out by walking, even just five minutes a day, and slowly build each day. Lay out your workout clothes the night before. Create a pattern in your habits that will eventually shape your mind until it becomes a routine.

I wake up at 4:15 AM every morning. I drink a glass of water, take my vitamins, put on my headphones, and lock into my meditation vlogs. I keep the house dark. I saturate my mind with positive messaging. When I start my day like this, I am setting myself up for success. I am laying the foundation for a great day.

Preparing your mind through mindfulness and meditation will help you find clarity before the chaos. We must find stillness in order to create and nurture a clear mind. A clear mind allows us to see more and visualize without clutter while giving us the opportunity to see the goal, feel the goal, experience the goal, and be the goal.

It is not unlike a writer leaving their home for a quieter space to be free of distractions or the student who goes to the library. Wherever you can find a quiet place in your mind, go there. To move forward, you must start, and by doing, one small step at a time, you will soon find days, even months, have passed, and that one small tweak you made has now become something significant, perhaps turned into an unbreakable habit.

The early morning has become a ritual, it is my "me" time. I try not to miss this part of my day, ever. It's my favorite time of day. I do not check my cell phone. I don't check emails. It's a sacred time that belongs 100% to me. I know this habit is preparing me for a winning day. In the end, every day is another opportunity to start fresh, so do not beat yourself up or be discouraged if you miss your routine. Simply reset, restart, and get back on track.

Here are a few actionable steps to get you on your way and Locked In:

James Clear, the author of the #1 New York Times bestseller Atomic Habits, suggests breaking things down into small, actionable tasks. He frames habits as the "compound interest of self-improvement," highlighting how small, incremental changes, when repeated consistently over time, can lead to significant results. He illustrates this with the example that getting 1% better each day for a year results in being 37 times better by the end of the year. As in one of my all-time favorite books, the *Compound Effect*, Darren shares the principle that small, consistent, daily actions, positive or negative, accumulate over time to produce massive, exponential results. It argues that success is not due to overnight breakthroughs, but rather mundane, daily disciplines sustained long-term. Key components include choices, behavior, habits, and time.

I believe in putting yourself on autopilot. Through repetition, that action will become a habit. Repeat it over and over until it sticks. Famous soccer star Cristiano Ronaldo follows an exceptionally regimented daily routine, combining a strict diet, disciplined workouts, and focused recovery sessions. He even naps five times a day, each for 90 minutes, as part of a polyphasic sleep cycle, rather than sleeping for eight hours straight at night. This approach is designed to maximize muscle recovery and enhance alertness.

That's what true preparation looks like, approaching both the game and the fight of your life with unwavering, laser-focused dedication. Beyond personal discipline, success also requires surrounding yourself with positive, hardworking, thoughtful, and caring people who inspire and support you in reaching your goals.

What seems impossible can become possible with practice and repetition. What is it you've been wanting to do but assumed you could not? Take the first step today.

GOALS | Write It Out

- What do I want to accomplish today, this month, and this year?

____

____

ACTION | Move Forward

- What will I implement in my daily schedule to move one step closer to achieving my goals?

____

____

CONNECT | Who Can Help Me?

- Who can I ask to help me stay on track and achieve my goals? Is that person a coach, trainer, therapist, accountability partner, colleague, mentor, spouse, significant other, specialist or expert in a specific field?

____

____

Chapter 3

Daily Routines

"Your mind is a powerful thing. When you fill it with positive thoughts, your life will start to change." — Unknown

A daily routine is one of the most effective ways to build momentum. The key is to create both a morning and an evening routine, and stick with it.

What do top athletes and successful CEOs have in common? Take a page out of their playbook and you, too, can build a powerhouse morning routine that sets the tone for a winning day. It usually begins around 5 AM and before 9 AM with a well-planned morning routine. And the end of the day wraps up with a perfectly executed evening routine. In order to start the day out for success, with the right mindset, you must start the night before.

A couple of summers ago, during my August funk, I was neither inspired nor in flow. I had lost momentum. I knew I needed to reorganize my thinking. I had to get my mind right from the moment I got out of bed. My solution was to immerse myself in mindfulness blogs and various meditation practices. **With headphones in place, I locked in.** Not only was I immersing myself in daily vlogs and podcasts, penetrating my every thought, but I was also watching TEDx Talks to learn the key concepts between mindfulness and meditation. Now it's been many years since that melancholy morning that gave birth to what became one of my non-negotiable, daily rituals.

<u>Morning Routine</u>

Morning routines and daily rituals set the tone for the day. They prepare us, mentally and physically for what's ahead. They ground us before life begins to pull us in every direction. Early morning happens to be my favorite time of day. Did you know that TikTok videos tagged with #MorningRoutine have been collectively watched 14.6 billion times? One of the most common morning routines is called the #5to9, a reference to the hours between 5 and 9 AM when the highly motivated can put in four hours of chores and self-care before starting the workday.

Let's take a detailed look at a few of the daily routines of some of the most successful and high-functioning entrepreneurs of today: Tim Cook, Apple's CEO, starts his day very early, typically before 5 AM, and is known for a structured and disciplined routine. His mornings are characterized by a focus on email, exercise, and a healthy breakfast. Evenings are dedicated to relaxation, potentially including outdoor activities and reading, before an early bedtime to ensure sufficient sleep.

Michael Phelps focuses on diet, exercise, and mental preparation. And particularly during his peak competitive years, it was structured around rigorous training, focused recovery, and a carefully managed diet. He would wake up early for multiple swimming sessions, incorporate weightlifting and dry land training, prioritize sleep and naps, and consume a high-calorie diet to fuel his intense workouts.

David Beckham focuses his morning and evening routines around fitness, family, food, and sleep. He incorporates all aspects of his day around his family and their schedules. **Sundar Pichai**, CEO of Google, has a relatively calm and focused morning routine that includes waking up between 6:30 and 7 AM. His focus is reading multiple newspapers, a cup of tea, and a vegetarian breakfast.

Legend Kobe Bryant's morning routine began around 4:00 AM. This involved warrior breathing exercises (inhale for 4, hold for 4, exhale for 8) to calm the mind and prepare the body. He followed with joint rotations to wake up the nervous system, followed by core exercises (planks, hollow body holds, etc.) to activate the body. Morning cardio started at around 5:00 AM. Fundamental basketball skills were practiced, emphasizing repetition. He focused on specific techniques and deepened his skills. He maintained a strict diet, prioritizing protein and nutrient-rich foods like lean meats, vegetables, and whole grains.

My morning routine has become a non-negotiable activity, whether I am in town, in my LA home, or on vacation. I do not deviate from my routine. Prior to executing a formal morning routine, I would start working right away, checking emails and text messages, promoting our real estate listings, and planning my day. My morning routine has definitely evolved over the years, for the better.

Looking back, it was the pandemic that most likely created the need, desire, and urgency to change my life. We were fortunate enough as Realtors that our job was deemed "essential." Even so, the lockdown was difficult for someone so used to being out and about and then relegated to the confines of home, with more than ample time to ponder and obsess. If I may offer some advice, I would like to encourage you not to wait for the next pandemic to rearrange your life in order to position yourself for success. Begin today.

My daily routine is ever-evolving, refined with intention, guided by purpose, and activated in motion each day. I rise between 3:30 and 4:30 AM. If I sleep until 5 AM, that feels late. After I feed our cats, Riggs and Lini, I drink a glass of water and take my medications and vitamins. I usually add magnesium or electrolytes to my water. If I have a lemon, I squeeze that in, too. I locate my headphones and iPhone, keeping the lights off, as I am not ready to greet the day, as I have a calming morning routine to enjoy, and I prefer the darkness. Oftentimes, when I rise, the moon is still shining bright; I have witnessed some incredible full moons on many of those mornings. I go upstairs to our loft, lie down on our very comfortable cloud-like sofa, and listen to meditation vlogs with eyes closed. If you prefer, you can sit up with your legs crossed.

At this moment, I am locked in and in the zone. It's during this time that I relax and am inspired. Sometimes it is difficult not to sit up and jot down my thoughts, but I try my best to remain in position. Around 7 AM, I make coffee, with my headset in place. When my husband awakens, I usually put up my hand to let him know I am still locked into my morning routine and am not ready to let the day in. I do more often than not bring him his first cup of coffee. He prefers his coffee with the news, so I head back upstairs. Next, I may write down my thoughts in my iPhone Notes or in one of my many journals. I look for an empty page, as most pages are usually filled with past scribbles and inspired thoughts. I then recite a mental gratitude list, and of course, it always begins with my family. All my goals for success include my family as well. After a cup of coffee, I head downstairs to our gym, where I jump on the trampoline, ride the Peloton, or walk on the treadmill. A definite and self-proclaimed multitasker, I watch relaxing YouTube vlogs, toggling between meditation videos and beautiful places around the world, most often inspiring destinations throughout Italy, France, and St Barth. After that, I address text messages and emails, which is usually followed by meetings on the East Coast or abroad. I love working and collaborating with clients and colleagues on the East Coast; since I get up so early, I can pack much more into my day using that three-hour time difference. I can even bother my daughter if she chooses to engage!

<u>Now It's Your Turn</u>

Take a moment to jot down your current morning routine and waking time, then draft out your ideal morning routine, and if you desire, your new waking time. Even if you are unsure or not yet ready to commit, write it out anyway. That is the key to the Mindset In Motion Method™. Small, consistent progress is what moves the needle forward, you just need a little push to create momentum. Each step brings you closer to your goal.

Draft your plan today, review it tomorrow, and soon you might just be ready to commit. I have experienced this so many times in my life. The mere thought of having a podcast terrified me. But as I jotted it down, considered the possibility, and spent time researching it, my podcast materialized. It is as if I didn't have anything to do with it; the universe just kept pushing information and opportunities my way. The same goes for a morning routine. Just Do It. You will be happy you did, and I know it will change your life for the better.

<u>Evening Routine</u>

Preparing for a good day begins at night. In order to reap the rewards of a winning morning, you must prepare before you execute. It all begins with a well-planned evening routine. Nothing sets the tone for a productive, positive day quite like proper sleep, and nothing throws it off more than when we skip it. We all know how we feel when we do not get a good night's rest.

Do you have an evening routine? Jot down your ideal evening routine and stick with it. Repeat it nightly until it becomes a habit. My evening routine begins with all lights off and windows closed throughout the house. I pull on my cozy sweats and favorite beanie, place a glass of water on my bedside table, turn my phone ringer off, and place it in the other room. Sometimes I stretch on the foam roller, something I should do more often. My laptop is also in the other room. Don't get me wrong, sometimes an idea strikes, and I have to jump up and run to my iPhone or laptop to send myself a reminder note or release an inspirational thought, but I do try not to. A few ideas to inspire you: dim the lights, take a warm bath, light candles, play calming music, read a book, listen to a book, try deep breathing exercises, yoga, light stretching, or journaling.

Now It's Your Turn

Take this time to draft your ideal evening routine, and work to commit to both your new or revised morning and evening rituals. I'd love to hear how your new routines elevate your spirit and make a difference in your life.

"The mind is like a fertile garden—what you plant will grow. Plant positive thoughts, and you'll harvest a life of abundance." — Unknown

The Importance of Morning Routines and Daily Rituals

For some, the morning routine is not a preference, it is a discipline. It is a ritual protected from excuses and outside noise. When a person commits to a role, a team, or a goal, their mindset shifts from hoping for results to training for them. Productivity and success become outcomes of preparation, not chance.

A well-structured morning routine can significantly impact your productivity, well-being, and even long-term success. Here's why:

1. Increased productivity

- Setting the tone: The habits you establish at the beginning of the day significantly influence your mood, energy levels, and decision-making throughout the day.

- Reduced decision fatigue: By having a set sequence of actions, you reduce the mental energy spent on making small decisions, freeing up cognitive resources for more important tasks.

- Improved focus: Morning mindfulness practices and planning enhance concentration and reduce distractions, leading to better focus throughout the day.

- Enhanced energy: Activities like morning exercise boost energy levels, making you more alert and capable of tackling tasks. Recently, I've added qigong, lymphatic drainage exercises, and the vibration plate to my daily routine, all easily done in the comfort of your home.

2. Evidence and statistics on productivity

- Studies suggest a correlation between structured morning routines and higher income levels: People with a morning routine may earn significantly more annually compared to those without one.

- Successful people often credit morning routines: Many high achievers, from CEOs to athletes, attribute their success to their early morning habits.

- Higher self-reported productivity among early risers: Studies indicate that morning people tend to report higher levels of productivity compared to night owls.

3. Potential link to wealth and success

While correlation doesn't equal causation, the association between morning routines and increased productivity and success suggests a potential link to wealth accumulation. One article notes that 92% of highly successful individuals have a solid morning routine and that 88% of wealthy individuals dedicate at least 30 minutes daily to reading.

Are you ready to plan and commit to your morning and evening routines?

GOALS | Write It Out

- Identify two to three activities that I will add to my *morning* routine?

____

____

- What are two to three activities I will add to my *evening* routine?

____

____

ACTION | Move Forward

- What time will I practice my morning routine, and what time will I close the day with my evening routine? Be specific in order to stay on track. Clarity precedes results.

____

____

CONNECT | Who Can Help Me?

- Seek guidance from this book, YouTube videos, podcasts, and experts.

____

____

Routines are the *Believe* and *Activate* steps of the Mindset in Motion Method™ in daily practice. When you build a routine, you're telling yourself, "I believe this matters, and I'm going to act on it every single day."

"When we set clear boundaries — for ourselves and for others — we dramatically increase our chances of achieving our goals."

Chapter 4

Mentorship

"A mentor is someone who allows you to see the hope inside yourself." — Oprah Winfrey

When I decided to branch out from a rental agent to a full-time real estate agent, I was a little nervous, to say the least. Realtors are paid solely on commission. Although rental agents are also compensated on a 100% commission basis, a client looking for a rental is much more casual about where they are going to reside. More often than not, it is temporary and not life-changing. A person seeking to buy a home is an entirely different story. It is much more emotional to find their nearly perfect dream home where they may live for many years, even a lifetime, creating memories along the way. Not to mention, buying a home is one of the most expensive purchases most people will ever make in their lifetime.

At this juncture in my life, my husband and I were raising our two-and-a-half-year-old daughter, our first child, while pregnant with our second child, and had recently purchased our first home. A lot of firsts! A childhood friend's mother shortly thereafter became my mentor. She convinced me to come work with her at the company where she worked, which required even more changes. Panicked thoughts shot through my mind like fireworks. Where was I going to find my clients? I had curated rental listings and found tenants for our rental listings, but how was I going to develop sales contacts? And what was the best way to draft a winning purchase contract when the time came? As I always did, even back then, I followed her instructions to a tee. I did not deviate. I did exactly as she said. Her mentorship was more than I could have ever imagined, and the guidance and confidence she instilled in me became invaluable and set me up for success.

I have always had the mindset,

"If it isn't broken, don't fix it. There's no need to reinvent the wheel when someone else has already paved the way."

The result? I went on to become a top 10 agent at a company known for rarely taking on new agents like me. That experience proved to me that with the right mindset, determination, and work ethic, anything is possible.

Mindset is crucial when it comes to making big life decisions, achieving one's goals, even deciding to marry or divorce. You have to be all in, or you're out. A mindset of unwavering commitment to your plan is paramount. I believe working alongside a mentor is some of the best advice I can give. Shadowing, and working with a mentor is where you will gain your best insight. That's when you are truly *in the game!* The value of working in a field you are passionate about and learning from someone who is in the trenches day in and day out, has a robust network, and has the skill, experience, and knowledge to share is more valuable than a **$200,000 MBA**. Not that school is unimportant, but a mentor will provide you with the skills and on-the-job training you simply cannot find in books or through traditional education.

Now that you are ready to find a mentor, where do you begin? Start with who you know. Check with your parents, family members, or friends and ask who they might be able to introduce you to.

Here's a larger list to make it especially easy to follow when you are ready to launch.

- Start by joining Facebook groups or other online communities that align with your interests and goals. These spaces are often filled with people willing to share advice, collaborate, and mentor.

- Attend in-person networking events and meetups: Meetups and industry-specific events are perfect for forming authentic connections. Face-to-face conversations often lead to valuable mentorship opportunities. Participate in activities that may lead to the ideal mentor. Find out what hobbies and interests your potential mentor enjoys.

- Join a mastermind group in your desired field or area of interest.

- Attend health, wellness, fitness, and bio hacking workshops, events, and/or programs.

- Join a support group. Take time to find the one that is right for you.

- Interview experts in your desired field: Founders, CEOs, and leaders love sharing their journey. Ask thoughtful questions, listen deeply, and follow up with gratitude. This often opens doors to ongoing guidance, even job opportunities.

- Read and Give Back: Two great books to start with: *The Go-Giver* and *Givers Gain*. Embrace a mindset of giving. Send thank-you notes, share your mentor's work, and refer opportunities their way. Mentorship is a two-way street.

You've identified your mentor. You have a solid list. But where do you start? How do you approach your potential mentor?

Savor this quote forever and put it into motion often.

"In life, you will never know unless you ask. You must not be afraid of reaching out and simply asking."

The Power of a Single Conversation, or Chance Meeting

One day, an acquaintance reached out and said she wanted to talk with me. We had only met briefly before at a mutual friend's garden party. At that meeting, she had told me she had always wanted to meet me. Certainly flattered by her comments, I suggested we meet for coffee or lunch sometime.

Weeks, maybe even months, had passed. When she contacted me and said she wanted to speak with me, I did not ask any questions. I had no idea why, but it didn't matter. I am always open to a meeting and always curious where a conversation may lead. We set a date and met a month later at Starbucks across the street from my real estate office. For some reason, I had a feeling a casual lunch would be too distracting from what she may want to discuss. My intuition was spot on, as it usually is. We sat down, and I asked how I could help her. She began telling me about her situation and how she and her husband were divorcing amicably but were still living together, and how she felt stuck, and beyond that, she was seeking to grow her business.

With that, I stopped her and asked, "Do you really want my guidance and suggestions?" If so, please take out a pen and paper, as my mind will start firing off ideas. I also warned her that I talk very fast.

I provided advice, multiple contacts in her field, and extended an invitation to meet me in Los Angeles so I could show her around and introduce her to designer showrooms where I thought she might find employment while meeting shop owners who might be interested in collaborating. I let her know my second home just so happened to be right in the heart of the Design District and that I had many contacts in her field in Los Angeles. She enthusiastically accepted my invitation, and in less than one week, we were touring the LA Design District, where I made multiple introductions, took her to a design seminar at the Pacific Design Center, and later, sent her off to a Chamber event that evening, without me. I was exhausted from exerting so much energy making sure I did as much as I could for my new friend.

After that busy day, she was re-energized. She went from the defeated person I met at Starbucks to a person with bounce back in her step in less than seven days! The best part was witnessing the sparkle in her eye. And by the end of the day, together in LA, she declared she was, in fact, going to make the move to LA.

Not everyone sees things as clearly or is comfortable acting as quickly, but she felt it and had the courage and mindset to propel herself into motion. She was open to the magic when I showed her the possibilities. Her smile was my reward. I captured a photo midway through that day. What unfolded felt like magic, but it was the result of intention and belief.

Supporting Insight: Why Conversation Matters

According to research published by Harvard Business Review, the power of connection is one of the most significant predictors of long-term goal achievement. People who share their goals with *supportive* communities increase their success rate by over 65% . Add in regular accountability, and that number jumps to over 95%. .

That's not luck. That's neuroscience. Your brain craves movement and connection. And when you declare something out loud, you activate your brain's *reticular activating system*, which helps you filter your environment for opportunities that align with your goal. At the same time, when you share your goal, that is when it becomes real. By sharing your goal with a family member, friend, colleague, or the world, it is as if you declared it to be, and you work hard to achieve it. I am mindful of what I declare out loud because once I put a goal into the universe, I hold myself accountable to achieve it. Trust me, to sit down and write this book was no easy feat. I prefer movement to being sedentary. I employed the Mindset in Motion Method to complete it.

"Action is the bridge between your dreams and reality. Small steps lead to significant changes."

As I was building my podcast, my video coach, **Kim Rittberg** asked who I wanted to interview. She encouraged me to *just ask*. Those words stuck in my head and whirled around on auto play. She instilled in me the confidence to just do it. I reached out to vloggers on YouTube, one in England and another in Australia. Mentors can be anywhere in the world—keep your eyes and ears open. At conferences, I asked the top producers and high-achieving panelists who accepted. I was successful in interviewing bestselling author and speaker Bob Burg on the rebrand of my podcast, from "Mastering the Art of Real Estate" to a broader audience under the new name "Mastering the Art of Success," on my debut episode.

Originally, Bob and I connected on Twitter/X. I had commented on an inspiring post that resonated, and he responded. A few months later, I went to his website to find his contact information and sent off an email asking if he would be interested in being a guest on my podcast. I recall very clearly; it was a Sunday, and he responded right away in the affirmative! I was beyond excited and pleasantly surprised. The key is to ask. You do not know how someone will reply until you do. An impactful quote I learned from a previous guest, Rebecca Sekulich: "No means next." Those three words are powerful and provide excellent advice. Whether you are asking for help, requesting a favor, interviewing for a listing, a job, seeking a raise, or asking for an introduction, the key is to be clear about what you are asking for and simply move forward and ask.

Exercise: Now take a break, and take the time to write out the following: Identify Potential Mentors

- Write out your ideal mentors

- List those people within your network you can reach out to.

- Make a list of who you want to meet or connect with, virtually or at an in-person meeting.

- List where your mentors might be: chamber of commerce meetings, networking forums, events, workshops, charity fundraisers, membership clubs, Facebook group pages, even professional social platforms such as LinkedIn and Alignable, the list goes on. Online events oftentimes host in-person events as well.

- Identify colleagues, classmates, family, and friends who might have the perfect connection or suggestion for you. You must ask.

- Scroll through your social media platforms and identify who might be a good candidate.

Mentor Wish List: It can be a person or more general, like the name of a company, a team, a group, a firm, a therapist, an author, a wellness expert. Stumped? Ask Google, ChatGPT or your preferred AI platform. Don't skip over this exercise and leave it for another day. Execute now. Take Action and Implement!

____

____

____

____

Introductions Made By

____

____

____

____

Places To Meet My Ideal Mentor(s)

____

____

____

____

And before you reach out, do your homework ahead of time. Be sure to research each person you want to meet and learn more about the group or event you wish to attend.

Giving back is one of my core pillars, and it should be yours, too. Where that came from, I am not certain. Looking back, my desire to give back not only fueled inspiration and provided me with a full heart, but it also turned my gift into a business. I recall stumbling into charity work some years back. Nancy, one of my personal mentors, asked if I would join their charity organization. I was at home with my young children but was eager to get back to work. I thought this could be something I would enjoy in the meantime. I replied with a resounding "yes!" I was excited to be working on a project. I am very task-oriented, and the bonus was that I really loved working on behalf of the Children's Support League. Knowing my efforts went to raising money for children at risk was a wonderful feeling. I made so many like-minded friends along the way who shared my sentiment.

When we give, we get so much more back in return. I did not understand that when I was in it. I continue to give from the heart, and somehow it always comes back and manifests in some other way. Just another example of reverse engineering my life lessons and accomplishments.

What are you willing to give in order to get?

If you're new to an industry and reluctant to join a team, you're setting yourself up to receive 100% of nothing and will learn the hard way if you choose to go it alone and not align yourself with success for success. A smaller percentage of something is better than zero. When you work with a team, whether in real estate or another business, being part of a team with strong leaders will provide you with more knowledge in a shorter time, and you'll encounter fewer mistakes. Making the decision to work on a team or to shadow an expert, side by side, for a period of time is invaluable, not only for your business development and growth, but also financially.

Keep in mind, it can be daunting for a mentor. It takes a lot of energy to always be on. To have another person in your presence, sharing insight and information and answering questions, all the while trying to get their work done, can be mentally taxing.

One summer, I took on three interns. I felt that if I was exerting the energy, wisdom, and knowledge for one, I might as well take on three because the energetic output is the same. I really did enjoy the experience, as I love helping others, but afterwards I did feel as if a weight had been lifted. Keep that in mind when you begin working with your own mentor.

Having a mentor is very beneficial and will expedite your learning curve. Before you lean on a mentor, you must **surrender to being teachable and coachable.** If you're not teachable or coachable, success will be harder, and slower. When you stay open to learning and are open to implementing a new way of doing or thinking, you grow faster, gain more insight, and get where you want to go with greater clarity and confidence.

I recall writing my first few purchase contracts early on in my career. I asked my mentor how I should draft the offer I was writing in order to prevail in a multiple-offer situation. Our market is very competitive, so when making an offer on behalf of a client, you must write as competitive an offer as you can.

Here are a few things she shared with me as a new agent:

Limiting contingencies is a big one. Your buyer should be pre-approved at the offer price prior to making an offer; thus, there should be no reason to have a loan contingency. Second, if you and the lender believe the home will appraise, you will want to remove that contingency as well. The buyer, however, must feel comfortable with this. In this scenario, if the home doesn't appraise, the buyer would need to come up with a slightly larger down payment. As agents, we guide our clients into the best possible position to 'win' a home, while also educating each buyer to make the right decision for themselves. It is very important for a new agent to understand these responsibilities, as it is not typically something they would learn in a real estate classroom setting. Another possible contingency to remove is the home inspection contingency. In our area, sellers provide the disclosures up front in order to limit negotiations after a contract is entered and ratified. This enables buyers and their agents to have the time to do their due diligence up front in order to understand the condition of the home prior to making an offer. Should the buyer wish to obtain bids or understand anything beyond what was provided in the home inspection and disclosures presented, that is the time to do it if they wish to present a competitive bid and position themselves for success. This is one of the many reasons Realtors cultivate strong relationships with key service providers, and why those relationships are so important.

At first, I was leaning on my mentor and the relationships she had built over the years, and 35 years later, we have our own incredible service providers. We would not be as successful as we are without these close relationships.

Over the years, contracts have been edited and amended. One of the clauses provided a checklist of minor but irritating items a seller might not want to do or have to do when provided with multiple offers on his home. I recall a colleague who would always check the boxes, asking the sellers to provide window screens throughout the home, repair cracked windows, and the like. My mentor suggested I leave those boxes unchecked. So I did. Those lessons I learned from the get-go made all the difference in becoming a top producer my first year in sales! I am grateful to Connie to this day for all of her guidance. I never questioned; I just listened. Why reinvent the wheel?

Alex Hormozi didn't know exactly what he wanted to do, but he chose a path, invested in mentorship, learned fast, and never stopped evolving. He learned from their mistakes. He implemented and sat in on meetings he would never have had the chance to attend had he not engaged. Had Alex gone the traditional route, formal education, trial and error, without mentors or learning from those who had already been there, he would not be the successful person he is today. His journey is an incredible lesson in taking advantage of the wisdom and knowledge of those who are ahead of you. From there, no doubt, he had his own ideas and continued to grow, but the time saved to get to where he wanted was invaluable.

The Power of Mentorship: Guiding Your Path to Success

Rising athletes, business owners, entrepreneurs, and anyone going through a new chapter in their life need a mentor, someone who has been there before. You are not going to have all the answers, and that is okay.

Wherever you are in life, you don't need to have all the answers. You just need to know where to find them, and it all begins with a simple Google search, a few prompts typed into ChatGPT, a little research, and a few questions. And watch the world open up.

"One of the greatest values of mentors is the ability to see ahead what others cannot see and to help them navigate a course to their destination." – John C. Maxwell

When you give someone responsibility, they rise up to meet expectations. A good mentor will help you level up. As the mentee, you will need to put in the hard work and stay accountable. If you can do that, you will succeed.

"Mentoring is a brain to pick, an ear to listen, and a push in the right direction." — John Crosby

If you are seeking to get ahead in your studies, interview for a new job, move up in your desired career, find a soul mate, run a 5K or a full marathon, write a book, embark on a new venture, prepare and execute a TED Talk, launch a new business, lose weight, get fit, or reduce the stress in your life, MENTORS are a key component to your success. In life, many have come before you, and there will be many who follow long after, but while you are here and seeking to improve, level up, or conquer your desired goals, there is no substitute for a mentor. Oftentimes, it takes a kick in the behind to jumpstart your success and propel you forward.

Excuses, Excuses, Excuses—Be Bigger Than Your Excuses

I truly believe: "No" is not an option. Once I have an idea or someone asks for my help, I will work to make it happen. I often tell people, if you are not serious, do not ask me. Resistance can be real or imagined. Everyone has excuses. Novices think they can do it alone, but not many will.

Mentors: Here is my definition of M.E.N.T.O.R.S

- Mentors
- Elevate
- Novices
- To
- Overcome
- Resistance
- In order to achieve
- Success

Mentors Elevate Novices To Overcome Resistance In Order To Achieve Success

Now it's your turn to take action. Now that you have identified your mentor wish list above, what and how do you ask someone to mentor you?

Exercise: What questions do you want to ask? Be prepared before you reach out to your mentor. **Here are a few questions to consider. And add your own:**

- How did you get started in the business?
- Did you have mentors?
- What role did they play in your life?
- What were the roadblocks to getting started?
- What would you have done differently?

____

____

____

- **Exercise:** Make a wish list of things that you would like to accomplish, learn, and ask.

____

____

____

How to ask a mentor for their help, time, and guidance?

- Research your mentor(s).
- Reach out by email or social media.
- Make it personal.
- Share something they've shared.
- Compliment your potential mentor.

- Know what you're asking about and why this person.

- Be prepared to take notes.

- Respect their time.

Exercise: Reach out to five potential mentors with personalized messages via email, in person, phone, or social media. A simple search on Google or ChatGPT might help you locate their contact information or website, along with LinkedIn, my go-to, and Yellow Pages, for those old enough to remember telephone books.

____

____

____

What if they say no or simply don't respond? How might you deal with rejection and put it in perspective?

- Don't take it personally. In general, people are busy and just might not have the time. I do suggest reaching out a few times before you give up.

- 'No means next.' —Rebecca Sekulich. I think it's brilliant.

- If you're going to be successful in business, you must cultivate a thick skin.

Exercise: How many rejections did you get? How did that make you feel? Take the time here to journal your thoughts. The goal is to move through your emotions and *depersonalize the rejection.* Keep in mind that if you start with a good morning routine, you'll feel better, stronger, and more confident.

69

<u>GOALS</u> | Write It Out

- Identify potential mentors. Utilize your exercises above.

____

____

<u>ACTION</u> | Move Forward

- Take action, lock in, and lean into momentum.

____

____

<u>CONNECT</u> | Help One Another

- Mentorship is a two-way street. As the mentee, you will need to put in the hard work and stay accountable while being kind and helpful to your mentor, which will only help to foster your growth and success. How can I best serve my mentor?

____

____

Chapter 5

Find the Spark

"Stop waiting for inspiration. Ignite it." – Debbi DiMaggio

I was walking down the street after taking a new listing. I answered a call from a woman on the East Coast whom I had met at a celebrity gifting suite in LA. She told me where we had met, yet I could not place her but listened anyway. I had met so many people, as it is an all-day event where celebrities and their handlers, publicists, photographers, and other gifters stop by to meet you and learn about your product. At that particular gifting suite, my product was my second book, Mastering the Art of Real Estate. I recall it being an exhausting but fun day. She asked if I would help her with an Emmy event she was planning in Beverly Hills. My usual and automatic response was always a swift no. That was because I never wanted to leave my kids during their school years. Even when they were in high school, I always wanted to be there when I had a choice. I knew they would be heading off to college one day, so I took advantage of every moment. But this time was different.

I paused and thought to myself: both Bianca and Chase are gone, Chase in college and Bianca in Australia. I could actually do this. I remember that day so vividly. I said yes, I will. I figured I'd work out the details of who she was later. It's my nature to always be open to possibilities and opportunities. It is that spark I am always on the lookout for.

That afternoon, walking down the street, I picked up a phone call, not letting it go to voicemail. Had it gone to voicemail, and I not knowing who she was, I may have left the call unreturned. But I did answer that call, a call that became the spark that propelled me into my next chapter, which led to LA, right as the empty nest was crushing me. That one call ignited something in me that changed my life and gave me a new direction. That was over eight years ago. It was a pivotal moment that opened up a whole new world for me. It led me through doors I never knew existed, introducing me to new friendships, unforgettable experiences, and a journey that continues to unfold.

"When we open our eyes to what is possible, we never know what can happen. I refer to it as being on the lookout for magic and open to the possibilities."

As the story goes, I met my new friend in Beverly Hills. We rented a beautiful Airbnb across the street from the Beverly Hills Hotel. Before we checked in, we met up at the Polo Lounge. She was a bit overwhelmed, as she was in charge of planning and executing the Emmy Party with a sit-down dinner in a private home in Bel Air, and she was starting at ground zero. Needless to say, she was a bit panicked, so I ordered two glasses of champagne and took out a notepad and asked what she needed, trying to calm her nerves. "A photographer," she replied.

When I meet people, I typically enter their name and where we met, what they do, or something that will remind me who they are into my iPhone contacts. At one of the gifting suites, a photographer was stationed at my booth for the entire day. We exchanged contact information, and I programmed his name along with the designation, 'LA photographer.' While sitting at the Beverly Hills Hotel with my friend, I sent him a text message: "I am sure you must be busy as it is Emmy season, but in case you are available, we are seeking a photographer for an Emmy party in Bel Air." He responded, "I am actually free." That was easy, I thought. "What next?" I asked my friend. She said we needed auction items and one singular WOW item.

I told her that I had noticed an artist who has been traveling the world showcasing his art, which included painting his face and body and interviewing people he met along the way. I said, "We have nothing to lose. I will DM him."

I had certainly gained momentum as Thomas sent a text right back saying he had a sculpture and that he would be happy to donate. Both Thomas and the photographer showed up at the Bel Air estate at our walk-through and followed through on their promises even though they did not know us. It was quite amazing. I always follow my own advice: you never know until you ask; we have more to gain and nothing to lose. Having two yeses so quickly certainly made our job easier.

As I propelled myself through the empty nest and this new, uncharted territory, I focused on trying new things every day and saying yes more often than not. That single day, eight years ago, when I was walking down the street in Oakland, took that call, and said yes without hesitation, was the moment that launched me into motion. It would be the catalyst to carry me all the way to LA and back for more. It's a reminder: sometimes the most life-changing decisions happen in an instant. What's something you said 'yes' to that changed your trajectory?

I continued to meet people while in LA, even during that short weekend. And made friends that evening at the Emmy party in Bel Air, who I am still close with today, which led to new opportunities. I met two USC students who had reached out to me on Twitter. They asked me to produce their film. I messaged them back and let them know that I was a Realtor and had no idea what went into producing a film. His reply was brief yet poignant. He told me a producer did many of the same things I do as a Realtor. It was just a few weeks after the Emmy party when I met James and Sam and agreed to produce their film. When we met to hear their pitch, I realized I didn't really care what the film was about. The two young men reminded me so much of my son, Chase, and his friend Quinn who I had spent years cheering on from the sidelines, traveling across the country to watch their lacrosse games and driving them to summer camps. All I saw were two passionate young men serious about what they wanted to do, and that was all it took for me to say, "Yes!"

They ended up with an invitation to the Silicon Valley Film Festival, and to my surprise, as the credits rolled, there on the big screen in front of me was my name, **Debbi DiMaggio**, **Producer**, in big bold letters, standing alone! I could not get out my phone fast enough and missed taking the shot, but the image is embedded in my mind forever. Years have passed, and that young actor I once knew is now thriving. I was proud of him then, and I'm just as proud today, **James Morosini**. From USC to a successful career as a filmmaker and actor, it's been incredible to watch his journey unfold. The framed movie poster they gave me, which includes my credit as producer, hangs in my LA home to this day. A reminder yet again to be open to the opportunities and what is possible when you are available without questioning every little thing. I did not set out to make money on this journey. It was the experience of something new that piqued my interest, simultaneously giving me a purpose that helped me through a difficult time as I was transitioning due to the empty nest. It opened my eyes to something new.

Every great journey **begins with a spark,** an idea, a moment, a flicker of inspiration that ignites a fire within us. It can stem from a casual conversation with a friend or a mentor, a poignant movie scene, a lyric in a song that resonates deeply, or even the way someone expresses their unique style. Perhaps it's a moment spent sitting by a swimming pool, gazing into the vastness of the ocean, or inhaling the breathtaking beauty of a sunset or sunrise. Maybe it strikes you while looking out the window of an airplane, witnessing the expansive sky and the billowy clouds that seem to stretch to infinity.

Jack Dorsey once said that success is achieved through three elements: recognizing luck, embracing insanity, and committing to non-stop iteration. But what about you? What is that spark that inspires you to conquer your dreams and goals?

There was a moment when I was driving our son, Bianca's younger brother, Chase, to school. I hadn't written *Contained Beauty* yet, the book that eventually helped me work through the emptiness of the empty nest. I was depressed because Bianca was away at college. It was at that very moment I learned that it is actually when the first child leaves home that the empty nest sets in, not the last. That's when the pain sets in. We live in a very 'Leave It To Beaver' neighborhood with tree-lined streets and next-door neighbors; this is not the country. But as I passed my house to make a U-turn, I witnessed a flock of turkeys covering our front lawn. I drove around the block, and as I came back to my house, I heard a song—"Your Book Is Still Unwritten" by Natasha Bedingfield. I was contemplating what I would do with my life now that things were different. Our routines had changed. Activity in and out of the house was not the same. Things were unknown, questions began, and the void and vacancy I felt in my heart and home were overwhelming.

But those lyrics stuck with me: "Your book is still unwritten." Words that later ended up in my book, *Contained Beauty, Photographs, Reflections, and Swimming Pools*. Those words are just another message, another spark I ruminated on for years, through the writing of *Contained Beauty, The Art of Real Estate, 52 Ways to Achieve Success in Real Estate*, multiple gifting suites, and in saying 'yes' more often.

> **"Every day, we all have the opportunity to write, rewrite, and edit the chapters in our own book."**

How do I want to write or rewrite my own book? What does my next chapter look like? Take a moment and jot down a few notes and thoughts.

____

____

____

Three years later, when Chase went to college, I was even more traumatized. Not only did Chase go off to college, but life as we knew it seemed to follow him right out that door, too. From his large friend group to lacrosse and football games, and everything else that goes along with having a family and raising a teenager.

I wandered around our empty house. I just could not live there anymore. Everything reminded me of the kids and the many wonderful moments, parties, and family gatherings. The house was empty; the pool was empty. Not literally, but figuratively. I knew I had to figure things out. What was I going to do? I needed an outlet.

I thought about it all the time. I knew I didn't want to play bridge or golf, like my friends, but I knew I had to come up with something. I tried many things. One of which became known as '100 Days of the Empty Nest,' where I thought up something new to do every day and recorded it on Instagram. I launched myself into motion each and every day. I had to first come up with an idea, and next, I had to implement whatever it was I was going to do. When we are stuck, the only way to get unstuck is to get moving and put yourself out there, and that's what I did. While I was experiencing sadness and loss, that pain eventually turned into a positive experience, and so much transpired not only for me but also for those I inspired along the way.

It was the spark that moved me out of my daily downward spiral that would usually hit when I came home at the end of the day to an empty house. #100DaysOfTheEmptyNest became my outlet. Some days I came up with big outings like attending a polo match in Sonoma or lunching in the Napa Valley; others were more adventurous: kickboxing, hip-hop dance, and even an aerial fitness class. It takes quite a bit of strength to climb those ribbons! But I was committed, my mind occupied, and it was also enjoyable.

"Turn your private pain into a shared experience through storytelling and lead by example."

That is just one example of why social media is so popular today. The world can be a lonely place, so when we share a personal story that others have experienced, or even something similar, it validates their feelings and makes them feel good about themselves and not so alone.

Some fun and interesting things came from my personal '100 Days of the Empty Nest' journey. A married couple, inspired by my posts, started taking kickboxing classes, and shared their happy photos. Another person following our adventures reached out and asked us to consider selling their winery and estate property. So we took a detour, from LA to Paso Robles before heading home in order to meet the couple, and ended up listing their property.

When Divorce Became Her Breakthrough

Over the years, we've witnessed many divorces, some expected and others quite unexpected. One of the best outcomes I have enjoyed watching has been the transformation of women friends who went through divorce, a very low time in their lives, only to rise up, propel themselves into motion with a new attitude and a rock-solid mindset to accomplish great things. Looking back, I know divorce was difficult for each of these women, but what they achieved and are doing today is admirable and extraordinary!

"You don't need to wait for something terrible to happen before you make something positive happen. You can be in a good situation and still create something extraordinary."

Whether beginning something new, stepping into your next adventure, or reluctantly stepping into your next chapter after divorce, death, or a relocation, you have to start somewhere. Once you push yourself into motion, momentum can't help but sweep you forward. Inevitably, you will meet new people, enjoy new experiences, and learn valuable lessons. What started out as a traumatic experience turned into something magical, even inspirational? I received text messages and calls from people who wanted to join in on the fun. It feels really good when you inspire another person to get into motion and enjoy another side of their life.

After the first year of going to and from LA and staying in hotels, I eventually moved into a place with my new LA friends. Years later, after settling into my second home, and new community, I mentioned to a new friend that I had been seeking a charity to get involved with. Logistically, it had to make sense, and I preferred a charitable cause rather than a business organization. I was eager to expand my circle of friends while simultaneously giving back and doing what feeds my soul. I also believe when you are doing something you enjoy, the result is that you will meet like-minded people, people with the same energy and heart.

My friend Elena connected me with a wonderful charity organization led by a most passionate, dedicated, and caring person. The cause, or "The Race to Erase MS." It took time and research, but I kept asking around, and eventually it happened. Beyond making new friends and being a part of the auction committee, the gala was a huge success, raising over $1,000,000. But beyond that, you would not believe who the closing band was. Yes, you guessed it, Natasha Bedingfield. And yes, she belted out 'Your Book Is Still Unwritten.' Coincidence? I think not. Accidentally on purpose, yes.

At least 8 years had passed since that morning in Piedmont when I was returning home after driving Chase to school to find a flock of turkeys covering our lawn. I recall the sadness in my heart, while at the same time, when 'Your Book Is Still Unwritten' played on the radio, I felt a glimmer of hope, a bright light in a very dark tunnel.

When we move into a new chapter, due to a traumatic event or something you chose, from experiencing a change, moving, starting a new job, the empty nest, a divorce, loss of a loved one, quitting a bad habit, or starting a new venture or hobby or going back to school, each of these changes requires space and time to think and contemplate. Certain situations may force us to be alone, which at times can be great, but you do not have to go through a traumatic event in order to create space and time to find inspiration and introspection.

The Contagion of Inspiration

All the things I was implementing during '100 Days of the Empty Nest' were to help me heal, while at the same time, I loved the fact that I was inspiring others. As I was in motion, doing whatever I was doing that day, I was not only having fun, it became contagious.

When you are doing what is enjoyable to you, you may inspire others along the way. Not that they want to mimic you, but you inspire them to find joy in their own life. People love to be a part of a movement. It may be something as big as a political movement, a part of a trend, or a TikTok challenge. It's the spark that ignites a fire. That spark might come from someone else, but it's contagious, it jumps from one person to the next. It can be a dance that takes off like the Macarena or a trend that goes viral like the Bucket Challenge; inspiration is contagious. Whether it was something you saw on TikTok or Instagram or something that inspired you on the streets, in a movie, or on a podcast.

- Seek inspiration

- Be on the lookout for magic

- Possibility creates opportunities

- Ask yourself, What is something fun I want to try or do?

I challenge you to find time and space in a day or a week when you are *happy* and see what transpires. When we allow time in our schedules to do nothing, that is when inspiration hits. It can be a room in your home free from distractions, or you can go to a park, for a walk, or to a coffeehouse so you are not tempted to start cleaning or all the many things in our homes that steal our attention. Whatever that place is for you, find it, and allow yourself the freedom to imagine and to think while your thoughts permeate and opportunities materialize.

When you give yourself time and space, you never know what might open up for you. You have to be willing to listen, willing to say yes, and willing to take the first step. I know when I go to LA, I am away from my usual routine, which is a home full of stuff, closets to clean, and things I could be doing. Often, I find myself rearranging the furniture. In LA, I have fewer distractions and a different perspective, and I make time to sit in places where I do not know anyone, like cafes or parks, where I can sit, write, work, and contemplate. I might go for a long walk or sit on a beautiful rooftop, locked in with my headphones on. Sometimes I play music; other times I am blocking out the noise.

Most people have to hit rock bottom or are thrown into a traumatic event, which becomes the thing that forces them to pivot, and that event is the catalyst to moving the needle forward and doing something life-changing. However, you do not have to hit rock bottom before you rise to the top.

Sometimes we need space apart from others, alone time. If you aren't getting along with your spouse and are miserable, before it gets any worse and there is no way back, try to spend some time apart to see how you feel. Don't allow your unhappiness to fester, or wait too long before you take action. Maybe you can even save your marriage. One of you will have to broach the subject, but you both know you're not getting along, so try a little space and see what transpires. At least you are giving yourselves a fighting chance.

Clearing the Clutter

Just clearing the clutter in your home helps clear the clutter in your mind. Clearing the clutter from our environment allows new ideas to flow. As I write this passage, I am in the process of cleaning our loft, where I kept bins of real estate paperwork behind the couch. The garage and my closet are next! On a recent episode of 'Mastering the Art of Success,' while interviewing Emma J. Carter, a professional organizer, it was during that interview that I committed myself to hiring her.

Challenge

In your own home, create space consciously by decluttering your environment in order to open up your mind and be inspired. Clearing the clutter helps to reduce stress, increase our focus, and improve our mood. A cluttered environment can increase cortisol levels, contribute to feelings of being overwhelmed, and negatively impact sleep quality. Conversely, decluttering creates a calming, organized space, provides a sense of accomplishment and control, and can even boost creativity and productivity.

You can fill the space you create with anything you want, both positive and negative. It is important to consciously fill that space. If you don't consciously fill that space with what you want, it'll fill up with random stuff. And often with negative stuff. The goal is to focus our attention and make deliberate, complex decisions about our space and what we fill it with.

Making the Covid Pandemic Fun

The pandemic was an awful time in our history, no doubt, but similar to disasters of the past, good things to come from difficult times, as well. During the pandemic, we had nothing but time and space. Time to think and space to be filled. Depending on what you chose to fill the space and time with, we all had different experiences. I knew I would go crazy being home all day. Thankfully, Realtors were deemed "essential workers," but we could not work all day, so I found various outlets to stimulate my mind and body.

First, I set out to create an in-home spa. I purchased a foot massager, an infrared detox blanket, and an LED mask. I had a manicurist come to the house, as well as a masseuse; both came properly protected. I recreated my outside life indoors.

Next, I took up baking. I rarely, if ever, cook. I have only baked a handful of times in my life. What transpired was very unlike me, but I knew at some point in the day, I had to stop working on my real estate business and take a break. One day, I just started baking. My goal was to bake 19 items for COVID-19. Every day I'd stop working, pick a recipe, and bake something. Usually, I would post each step from beginning to end, posting photographs and videos on Instagram stories.

Obsessed with branding, I came up with what I thought was the perfect name: the 'Well Heeled Baker.' A perfect blend of my sense of style and baking. It not only provided a definite break from work, but also because if you are a baker, you know baking is a science; you must be precise with each ingredient. This newfound hobby also nurtured connection and interaction with my viewers. Long after COVID, I loved hearing from friends who asked me to bring back the *Well Heeled Baker*. But I do not know who that person is any longer. She ceased to exist, and I haven't been motivated to bake again since. I really did enjoy it while I was doing it. It filled a vacancy, a void.

Baking during Covid gave me the opportunity to take a break from work, a much-needed diversion while at the same time filling the time and space with a positive, fun, and enjoyable experience. It is up to you to be happy or sad, positive or negative, distressed, depressed, or inspired. How are you going to change your attitude and get into motion? What will you do to get yourself moving forward and into action?

Prompt

Open your mind, walk through new doors, seek inspiration, observe, and explore. Use your imagination. Allow your mind to wander. What would be enjoyable for me to do today? I understand if you are down and in a funk, it's difficult to answer. But if you keep asking that question every day, you can eventually pull yourself out of anything. It is quite liberating to allow your imagination to run wild and fill the space with positive experiences that cultivate inspiration.

Baking might not be your thing, but there are so many wondrous things you can do. Here are 10 things you might try to fill your mind with positive and nurturing thoughts.

- Exercise
- Meditation and Mindfulness
- Journaling, Vision Boarding
- Reading
- Yoga
- Sound bath
- Qigong
- Taking a bath
- Deep breathing
- Lock In: Close your eyes and listen to music with your headset

<u>Be On The Lookout for Opportunities</u>

I once told my publicist, "Every morning when I wake up, it feels like Christmas morning. I never know what opportunities you have in store for me." It was an exciting time. One day it was an editorial interview; the next it was a live news interview. She also made introductions to magazines and news outlets who gave me space to write my own editorial pieces.

"By believing in possibility, you shift your perspective from "why bother" to "what if," which expands your horizon."

Open up your mind to stimulate new ideas. Allow yourself to dream. Use your imagination. Look for ideas from what is around you. Look for signs, whether it's in a conversation or something you see. It may be a word, lyrics in a song, or something that popped into your mind. Be on the lookout for signs. Inspiration can come from anywhere: an old building, beautiful architecture, an exquisite painting, even a conversation, or a look. You are seeking those aha moments. Find a quiet place where you can be alone with your thoughts and allow ideas to permeate.

Exercise: Make a list. Jot down ideas, and write out what it is you want to do, achieve, or accomplish. The Spark That Ignites a Fire: I encourage you to look for the magic in your everyday life. My hope is that you will use this blueprint to harness that spark within you. Keep a journal with inspired thoughts, and enjoy the journey.

<u>**GOALS | Write It Out**</u>

* Jot down ideas and things I want to do.

____

____

<u>**ACTION | Move Forward**</u>

* Find time and a quiet place to think and write. Lock in and dream!

____

____

<u>**CONNECT | Who Can Help Me?**</u>

* Do I need further guidance? Or do I just need to alert those around me that I am taking the time and will be back?

____

____

Chapter 6

Planning

"Without directions and a clearly defined map, we cannot arrive at our destination."

During the COVID pandemic, I was chatting with a longtime friend. I asked her if she had completed her book. She said she hadn't. It had been nearly twenty years since she started writing it. As I got to speaking with her, she had so many roadblocks and barriers that it was clear she was not going to finish the book on her own. This is not an uncommon story. A significant majority of people, 92% of those who set a goal, ultimately fail to achieve it. My friend was no different. But I knew it was important to her.

I told her that if she was willing, I would meet with her on Zoom once a week, and I'd hold her accountable to complete her weekly assignments. I notice in retrospect, now as a coach and mentor, how different I was as a mentee. Without question, I accepted and implemented what my mentors shared with me. As I began coaching my friend, I was struck by how many self-imposed barriers stood in her way, each one needing to be dismantled before she could truly move forward.

Coaching is not unlike what we do as real estate advisors; we often double as psychologists. It was not simply getting her to put pen to paper. I also had to work with her on breaking limiting beliefs, adopting a success mindset, and overcoming cultural barriers. Once we started working together, within four or five months, she was able to complete her book and move through additional hurdles before going to print. We began by breaking down and establishing our goals. The first item on the agenda was to work through each chapter until completion, one week at a time. Implementing a deadline was key. Without a deadline, time passes all too easily.

As a writer, I know too well the desire to edit until the sentence, the paragraph, and the chapter are perfect. But perfection is a myth. The next task at hand was finding someone with the time and desire to read her book and make edits. Among the more straightforward steps was connecting her with my publishing company, securing an ISBN identifier, and streamlining the process so that everything, from cover design to printing and distribution, would be ready when the time came. However, it was the emotional side of the equation where she put on the brakes, allowing fear, doubt, and hesitation to slow her forward motion. The more difficult issue, in her mind, was overcoming how her parents, more specifically, her father, would react to the book. Many family members resembled personalities in the book, as well as their strong, male-dominated cultural traits.

I remember vividly when the books were scheduled to be delivered to her home; it just so happened to coincide with the timing of her parents' visit that same week. She created an elaborate tale about what was in the boxes and whose boxes they were. My question to her was, "Now that you have waited nearly 20 years, are you going to wait until your father passes away before you go to print?"

Another barrier she had to overcome was her fear of going public. I told her an author must go public with their book if they want readers. I was able to convince her to create a Facebook group page and begin reaching out to friends, as well as the many groups she had been a part of throughout her lifetime. She was creating a network, an audience, and bringing them together under one roof. By the time of the printing, she had blossomed. She was much more open to listening, learning, engaging, and implementing. That is when I planned and executed her first two book signings in California. (She lives in Utah.) From there, she was officially out! It was magnificent to witness and to have a small part in her success. The greatest reward and greatest pleasure in coaching is to watch your client soar to heights they never thought possible.

Did you know that having an accountability coach, partner, or mentor will not only help you achieve your goals but also statistically give you a 95% success rate? "What would you do if you knew you could not fail?" When I coach, I often ask this question. It is truly remarkable how many people pause, unsure whether their dreams are even possible. But every success story starts with belief, not in perfection, but in possibility. This is why the first two steps in the Mindset in Motion Method are to have a goal and to believe. You must have a goal, or a dream, and believe you can achieve it. What is the harm in dreaming?

The Mindset in Motion Method is a powerful five-step process, reverse-engineered from goals I achieved, so that I could share it with you. My goal is for you to implement the Mindset in Motion Method to conquer your own goals.

Change is the only constant in life, and yet, it's often the hardest thing to navigate. Whether you are considering a career change, downsizing your home, or seeking a fresh start, changing your habits can feel daunting. Having the right attitude and the right mindset can make all the difference. I developed the *Mindset In Motion Method* to help people like you embrace life's many transitions with clarity and confidence.

The Mindset In Motion Method™ is built around five powerful steps:

1. **Goal**: Clarify. Identify and envision the life you want without limits.

2. **Believe**: Affirm. Strengthen your mindset to overcome doubt and fear.

3. **Internalize:** Write it out. Align your thoughts and habits with your vision.

4. **Share**: Announce. Surround yourself with supportive people who lift you higher.

5. **Activate**: Take consistent, courageous action to create lasting change.

Your next chapter doesn't have to be uncertain, it can be intentional, inspiring, and exactly what you've been waiting for.

1. Goal

Start by dreaming. Define your goal clearly; it is only in clear waters that we can see below the surface.

"No one can see their reflection in running water. It is only in still water that we can see."
— Zen proverb

Your goal should be something that resonates deeply within you, a dream that inspires and motivates. Did you know that setting a goal makes you approximately 43% more likely to achieve it, compared to not setting one at all? Putting pen to paper and writing down your goals increases your chances of achieving them by 42%. And if anyone ever tells you your dreams are silly, remember there's a millionaire walking around who invented the pool noodle.

"The Dream Is Free. But The Hustle Is Sold Separately." —Tyrese Gibson

2. Believe

"Believe you can, and you're halfway there." — Theodore Roosevelt"

Give yourself permission. Cultivate a strong belief in your ability to achieve this goal. Trust that you have the potential and resources necessary to make your dream a reality, even if you are not yet sure that you do. You must believe in yourself. To *believe* is to accept something as true, real, or possible, even without having complete proof. It's an act of trust, conviction, and a growth mindset.

> ***"A dream, like a plant, must be watered, fed, and nurtured in order for it to grow."***

Your mind will always believe everything you tell it. Feed it faith, feed it the truth, feed it with love, and don't get up until you believe it. Having the idea and believing in it is about percolation. It is what's bubbling inside of you. You must understand that what you do today creates your tomorrow, so don't waste precious time.

> ***"Life will only change when you become more committed to your dreams than you are to your comfort zone." — Billy Cox***

3. Internalize

Make the goal a part of your daily mindset. Embrace it fully, allowing it to influence your thoughts and emotions positively. Create a vivid mental picture of yourself achieving your goal. **Engage all your senses to make this vision as real as possible, reinforcing your motivation.** Here's where you want to connect the emotions of the heart with the mindset of your head, by creating neuropathic ways to generate momentum and energy to realize your dream. There are many ways to do this. But the strategy is through repetition in order to create a routine that becomes so easy and familiar that it becomes a habit. You might do this through gratitude practice, mindfulness, meditation, journaling, visualization, creating vision boards, and anything else to affirm and embed your goal.

Selling homes for over 35 years, I have many stories. I recall one instance where I had been showing our clients quite a few homes. We made a few offers but could not outdo other bidders. However, right before we made an offer on this one home, I took a photo of our clients in the living room. A few days later, our sweet, soon-to-be newlyweds prevailed! That's the power of internalizing a vision. That is manifestation at its core.

It is also how I manifested the home we live in today. My husband and I happened to see a home during the Broker *Tour* at different times, and while having dinner with my parents that evening, we were sharing our day. Not only had we both toured the home but it struck us personally, not just as agents on tour. The home needed lots of work, but the location and views were irreplaceable, so we moved on it. The first time we made an offer on the home, we competed in multiple offers, we lost, and the home went pending. One would think it was over. But not me. For some reason, I would not let go. I truly believed it was our home. We were not even looking to move. A few weeks later, I called up the listing agent to ask about the status of the offer. She shared that it had just fallen out of escrow. So, we drafted another offer. What I did not know was that the second time we were yet again in a multiple-offer situation. (The listing agent was not local. She did not disclose who was writing and how many offers she had coming in, as is customary in our market). We were shooting in the dark.

After a week of negotiations, we eventually prevailed. I have not known a story quite like ours. I believe I manifested this home through unwavering belief, intentional desire, and the daily practice of internalization. When I look back on how I manifested my home, I realize it wasn't through wishful thinking or chance, it was through **internalization**.

> *"Manifestation is belief. Internalization is identity. When your thoughts, emotions, and actions align with your vision, it stops being a dream and starts becoming who you are."*

The process began when I allowed myself to *feel* what living in my ideal home would be like. I didn't just create a Pinterest vision board or scroll through listings. I imagined waking up in this particular space filled with light, energy, and peace. I pictured the flow of the rooms, the view, and the smell of morning coffee in my kitchen. That vision wasn't a fantasy, it became a *familiar feeling*. Each day, I internalized that sense of belonging. I carried it with me, not as something I hoped for, but as something I was already connected to. These weren't random actions.

They were signals to the universe, and to myself, that I was ready. Each decision reflected the inner belief that my new home was already on its way.

Internalization isn't passive. It's about *living as if*, making decisions and taking steps from the mindset of someone who already has what they desire. If you decide to try it, you might begin clearing out clutter, organizing finances, and driving through neighborhoods that resonate with your vision.

Internalization bridges thought and action. It's the moment where belief transforms into behavior. Once my thoughts and emotions were in harmony with my desire, opportunities started to unfold naturally. That specific home appeared to feel right. We had not been looking at homes; it was the only home. The process, though not without challenges, felt guided and aligned. Because I had already internalized the outcome, I could move through uncertainty with calm confidence rather than fear.

Manifestation aligns with your Believe stage because belief is the *spark* that ignites creation. It's the moment when a dream moves from imagination into energetic reality, when you begin to *feel* it as real as possible, real, and already on its way.

Belief transforms desire into conviction. It shifts the mindset from "I hope this happens" to "I know this is happening." That emotional certainty, trusting that what you desire already exists, is what most people describe as manifestation.

In the Mindset In Motion Method™:

- Dream initiates the vision.

- Belief energizes it through trust and emotion.

- Internalization is where belief evolves into identity.

Manifestation is the **Believe** stage of the Mindset in Motion Method. It's when your dream shifts from imagination into energetic form, when you truly believe it's already yours. But internalization takes it further. It's when belief becomes identity. You live, act, and think in alignment with that belief until it transforms into reality.

I did the same with my life in LA. After years of work with a network care professional,* I was able to create a life in LA as a second place of residence. People and opportunities presented themselves to make it happen. It did not happen overnight. It took work, and I was committed. It's been over six years since I have had my second home in LA and a life filled with friends, work, charity groups, and an array of new experiences. Network Care Chiropractic, also known as <u>Network Spinal Analysis (NSA)</u>, is a gentle form of chiropractic care that uses light touches to the spine to help the body release stored tension and improve its ability to self-correct. It focuses on enhancing physical, mental, and emotional wellness by cueing the brain to reorganize the nervous system and develop new strategies for healing. The process, called an "entrainment," is a collaborative "dance" between the practitioner and patient that encourages the body to release stress and tension, leading to increased well-being.

When I was younger, I did not understand what I was doing or how things that I wanted seemed to happen. I recall thinking very hard and seriously about what it was. Not until many, many years later did I understand there was a term for my positive thinking and willing something to happen. What exactly is manifesting? Our creative power lies in our ability to transform the energy of our thoughts into material form. Manifestation begins with a single intention. One clear thought, aligned with belief and focus, becomes the seed from which new realities are born. Now, once you feel good about your goal, it is time for principle 4, to share it.

4. Share

According to a 2007 study by Dr. Gail Matthews at the Dominican University of California, you are 42% more likely to achieve your goals simply by writing them down. However, the success rate is even higher for those who take additional steps. One has a 43% success rate for those who only thought about their goals. And, a 76% success rate for those who wrote down their goals, created an action plan, and sent weekly updates to a friend. The magic lies in writing down our goals and sharing our goals with supportive people. By putting pen to paper, or fingers to the keyboard, we experience enhanced clarity, an increased commitment, better focus, improved memory, and greater accountability.

The key is to share about your goals with confidence and share your aspirations with *only* supportive people, affirming your commitment and reinforcing your determination. When we share our goals, we are more likely to hold ourselves accountable. Depending on the goal, you might share your goal with an accountability partner, a family member, a mentor, a coach, a boss, a partner, a therapist, or, if you are really bold and do not want to fail, you can share it on social media.

When we share our goals, we hold ourselves more accountable. Saying it out loud is a declaration, a commitment to act. The moment we share, our dream begins to take shape in the real world.

In the past, I have shared my goal to get back into my exercise routine. Sharing publicly and on social media provides reinforcement. Announcing your goal publicly gives us even more motivation to succeed. While documenting your journey by writing it down (in a journal or on Instagram) and witnessing your progress reinforces the positive behavior. Not to mention, the bonus spark is one's personal goal and public intention to get fit, may just inspire someone else. And that is well worth the risk of not achieving my goal. Sharing creates energetic momentum. When we tell someone what we intend to do, we subconsciously affirm that we *will* do it. It's no longer just a quiet wish. It becomes a promise we've made, to ourselves, to the people who believe in us, and to the universe. Accountability through sharing also builds connection. It attracts support, encouragement, and opportunities that might not have appeared if we had kept our goals private.

I wrote a blog years ago about eating healthy and dressing up even when you don't feel like it. Mindset in Motion was not yet hatched, but that blog follows the same line of thinking. I wrote about the importance of getting up, getting dressed, and getting out even when we don't feel like it. The sheer momentum in taking action propels us into a different and usually better mood. When in motion, we have the chance to change up our mood and experience something new, rather than sitting at home sulking.

It's the same when we're not eating healthy. When we make poor food choices, we don't feel great. But when we choose the right foods, we feel much more energized, both in mind and body. Dressing up instead of throwing on sweats and a hoodie can also brighten up your day, but the smiles along the way from others will help boost your mood, too.

To this day, I recall a woman from my charity who commented on a social media post, thanking me for sharing. She said I inspired her to get dressed up even though she had been spending so much time in the hospital at her husband's bedside. At the same time, she started eating blueberries and better foods to boost her mood. I was so touched she listened, and it resonated with her. She went on to say, "Even though my husband did not know I was dressed up or even in the room, I felt so much better." The moral of this story is that when we share and the result is that we inspire another person that truly is a gift. So do share what's going on with you.

It is up to you to decide when you might share publicly, with one person, or with a chosen few. I chose not to share the fact that I planned to run the LA Marathon. I wasn't training, and I didn't want people in my ear who might be naysayers. I did not want dinner parties and gatherings to be turned into a Q&A about whether I could or would not finish. Nor did I want to be judged the month preceding the marathon or listen to opinions about how I should train, what I should eat, or a myriad of other topics around something I really knew nothing about. If I were listening to all the noise, I just may have been dissuaded from running the marathon.

I was turning sixty that year. It was my goal, and I would either succeed or fail, but I did not want to be bogged down with unwanted information or unwarranted opinions. My personal training was in the research and immersion into the lives of the men and women who train and fight for our country and all that they endure to stay alive. The marathon was much less significant than fighting for one's life, and that was the mindset I held until I crossed the finish line.

Not until I was a week away from running the marathon did I share it with my husband. I told him he needed to come to LA with me in case I needed some help, although I was unsure of what that could be. In the end, it was wonderful and a huge relief he was there to pick me up, as I could barely walk. After 26 miles, my thighs were screaming with pain. When I was running, I couldn't feel the burn, but when I stopped, that is when the pain set in. The top of my thighs were sore, it was a pain I had never felt before.

5. Activate

And now, drum roll please, the last and most powerful step to reaching your goal is to *activate*. This is where everything you've believed, internalized, and spoken begins to move forward with unstoppable ACTION. The following highlights real-life situations and demonstrates how to move into action, activate, and achieve your goals.

Divorce is unfortunately very common. I can't imagine how difficult it would be to go through a divorce. From watching friends and clients who have gone through a divorce, I know the wide range of emotions they experience, the ups and downs. It's as if you're on a roller coaster you just can't get off. No doubt, the activation step is not easy for them to tackle. Here are a few ways I might suggest based on my coaching, as well as through my experience with the National Association of Divorced Professionals. The NADP is a group I joined so that I could be better equipped to help my real estate clients as they navigate the murky waters of divorce.

Here are a few action steps a person can take:

- Surround yourself with supportive family and friends.

- Build your own personal divorce team: You might join a Facebook or other divorce group. Support groups of all kinds offer a plethora of information. Take what you learn and vet it yourself, but I am certain you will come away with new information or conversations that might reinforce what you were already thinking. I always say, "You don't know what you don't know until you know, so listen, learn, and ask."

- Align yourself with an excellent divorce attorney.

- Be sure you have professionals working on your behalf, not the same ones as your former husband or wife. Seek out your own financial advisor and trust attorney.

- Ask your friends or close colleagues to recommend a professional therapist who specializes in divorce. If you have children, they too should see a therapist. Children of all ages will need help processing the situation as well. Divorce is a family affair and it affects everyone in the family unit.

- Stay healthy. Consider hiring a personal trainer or establishing an accountability partner.

It's not easy, but if you align yourself with a knowledgeable and experienced team to support you and provide helpful advice, you will find it much easier than going through it all alone. When my daughter went off to college, I was devastated. I felt as if a limb was ripped off. I was so sad. I still had my son and all his friends at home, but our family seemed to shrink from 4 to 3. It was a strange feeling. I knew it was her time to move on, but it didn't help the loss I was feeling. And when my son left 3 years later, it was another shock to my system. No more red cups and sticky floors, no more Friday afternoon grocery store runs to stock the refrigerator for Chase and his friends, no more waiting for the kids to go to bed before we would. No more lacrosse games and the satisfying sight of him coming through the door after practice. These were painful losses. I had two choices: to remain weepy and sad or straighten up and figure it out! As I did, I figured it out. It is not always easy to activate. Sometimes you might not have the information or know how to get started. In other cases, you might feel so depressed or distraught that you are mentally and physically unable to begin. That is when you need to align yourself with those who can help. The goal in the activation period is to take meaningful steps that bring the dream into reality or to conquer your goals while staying true to your mindset and vision.

Example 1: Take my girlfriend's story, and apply the Mindset In Motion Method™.

	Sofia's Story
GOAL	Complete and Publish Her Book
BELIEVE	Embrace the belief in herself that she would finally finish and publish her book.
INTERNALIZE	The Knowing that her book was already in motion and that completion was not only possible but inevitable.
SHARE	Once we began working together she started sharing her progress with a few supportive people, slowly but surely.
ACTIVATE	Once she embraced the above principles, she was able to overcome her fears and self-limiting beliefs and complete these milestones. Her attitude going forward pivoted to a more positive, growth-mindset-focused outlook with one intention: to conquer her goal.

It was at that time that I knew she would do it and that incredible things were to come.

Example 2: Let's implement the Mindset In Motion Method™ to share the healing process of Alexander's addiction. You first met Alexander in the introduction. What I love about his story is how he understood the importance of the 4th principle, by sharing your goal ONLY with supportive people. If you recall, the older generation looked at alcohol addiction as a weakness. By looking at Alexander and his friends, you would not consider them weak. It was actually the first time I shared the Mindset In Motion Method™ with strangers. I was pleasantly surprised by how well it was received and understood. It was the spark that ignited a deeper, more meaningful conversation that one might not expect in a Russian bathhouse social club.

I also love the story of my husband's longtime friend, an aspiring real estate agent who wanted to quit her second job but was unable to, as her real estate career had not taken off. She'd been trying to launch for years, but it just wasn't happening. When she finally decided it was time to buckle down and realized she had to change both her mindset and strategy, she called me up, and we started working together. It was really wonderful to watch her grow. Yes, we had some obstacles and limiting beliefs to overcome, but that is why she hired me. For Jane, it was all about activation. She had a well-defined goal; she believed she could quit her second job and go full-time, but the challenge lay in her ability to focus, internalize that belief, and take action. Together, we worked through her self-imposed roadblocks and structured a daily and weekly plan of action to set her in motion.

"Nothing happens in still water; water needs ripples and waves to generate movement."

Once we did that, the ball was rolling, and momentum propelled her forward and into action! As a result, she quit her part-time job and went into real estate full-time! It really did not take long, in comparison to the wasted years prior, while she was trying to do it alone without a coach or mentor. Refer back to Chapter 4, one of the most important chapters in this book, and my best advice is that a coach and a mentor can take you farther, faster.

	Alexander	Jane
GOAL	Sobriety	Full-Time Real Estate Agent
BELIEVE	He believed he could	She believed she could
INTERNALIZE	He appeared to have the conviction	She still needed help convincing herself
SHARE	Understood he needed to share and be surrounded by supportive people, not those in his culture who believed he was weak because he admitted to having a problem with alcohol	She was talking about it with supportive people, and that is how we were connected. One evening at dinner, our mutual friend suggested once again that she coach with me

ACTIVATE	He surrounded himself with others in the same situation, which gave him strength and the tools. Attended AA meetings and even started his own program to help others in his community overcome their addiction while providing a supportive environment.	Met with me 1x a week and allowed me to hold her accountable during the week and on top of her assignments. She shared wins, and we worked on investing time as a full-time agent by showing up in her office daily, hosting gatherings for friends and clients, and hosting weekly open houses.

The following two personal stories of hardship and trauma align with the Mindset In Motion Method™.

Terry Healey: Resilience, Identity, and Living Fully

The Challenge

From a life when milestones were routinely met with success, to becoming a Homecoming Prince in high school, and later the Fraternity President at UC Berkeley, Terry Healey's world once revolved around confidence, connection, and possibility. That life changed abruptly with a cancer diagnosis that would alter his face, his identity, and his future.

What followed were more than 30 surgeries and long stretches of recovery, moments spent lying in a hospital bed confronting a reflection he no longer recognized. The frivolous titles and external validations that once defined him fell away. Everything Terry knew about life and living it to its fullest was taken from him in a single moment.

The Emotional Reality

In the beginning, Terry felt what any thriving young man, or any human being, would feel: shock, grief, fear, insecurity, and deep self-pity. The loss was not just physical; it was emotional, social, and deeply personal. Yet Terry was not alone. Family, friends, nurses, doctors, and eventually support communities surrounded him, offering strength during moments when he had little to give himself.

Over time, Terry worked through his grief and began to transform it. What once felt unbearable slowly gave way to gratitude. In his own words, he emerged a better person than he would have been had he not walked this path.

The Mindset In Motion Method™ in Action

Goal

Clarity changed everything. Once Terry defined his purpose, who he wanted to be and how he wanted to live, he found direction. That goal became his anchor, motivating him through surgeries, recovery, and reinvention.

Believe

Belief was essential in the early days. Terry had to believe he could endure, adapt, and continue embracing life. This belief allowed him to shift his attitude, find strength in uncertainty, and choose hope over fear.

Internalize

Terry became a strong proponent of the mindset tools that reinforce inner conviction. Visualization, vision boarding, gratitude practices, and journaling helped him internalize belief and remain connected to possibility, even during the hardest moments.

Share

Healing did not happen in isolation. Terry surrounded himself with supportive people –family, friends, medical professionals, and peer support groups. Sharing his journey strengthened his confidence and reinforced the power of connection.

Activate

Terry didn't wait for life to come to him. He took action. He went on to excel in business multiple times over, married, and became an author, speaker, and influencer. He stepped fully into life, not in spite of his challenges, but alongside them.

Achieve | The Outcome

Terry Healey's story reminds us that adversity is universal. Whether we face visible differences, illness, loss, or everyday obstacles, what defines us is how we choose to respond. Terry lives a full life by embracing each opportunity, and each obstacle, with a positive attitude rooted in gratitude. His journey is a powerful example of The Mindset In Motion Method at work and a reminder that resilience isn't about returning to who we were, it's about becoming who we're meant to be.

On Becoming Ellie

By the time Ellie was twelve years old, she had moved more than thirty times, lived in four different countries, spent a year and a half in refugee camps, and ran away from an abusive con-man father. I'm told that by then she suffered from severe nervous tics, anger issues, and thoughts of ending her own life. And yet, when I met Ellie, only through the pages of this book, I never would have guessed the magnitude of what she endured as a child.

What I encountered instead was a woman with an enormous smile, quick laughter, and bright, attentive eyes. Her presence is warm, almost disarmingly so. She makes people feel comfortable. Seen. Welcome.

How does that happen? How does someone survive a childhood stripped of the things we associate with safety and normalcy, the school playground, sleepovers, Girl Scouts or Brownies, the comfort of returning to the same classroom year after year, growing up with the same friends, speaking the same language, and living in the same neighborhood? How does one grow up without the quiet predictability of holiday traditions, without watching *Santa Claus Is Coming to Town* or *How the Grinch Stole Christmas* on repeat each December? Ellie's childhood was stolen from her. And yet, if you met her today, you would never see that little girl who suffered so deeply.

So how did she get through? In her mid-twenties, Ellie made a pivotal decision. Having learned about the power of the mind, she realized that while she had no control over the circumstances of her childhood, she *did* have control over how the rest of her life would unfold. She decided that she wanted to be happy. That decision became her North Star. It carried her through grief and anger. As she slowly released a victim mindset, she felt relief. Her despair and depression loosened their grip. She began to feel less powerless and more capable until she could at last live in joy. Her resilient mindset showed her a peaceful life, even though all she knew early on was chaos.

Ellie is a living testament to what it means not just to survive adversity, but to transcend it. She bears no visible scars on her face or on her heart. She is open, generous, grounded, and free. She embraced a *Mindset in Motion* attitude, never stagnating, always growing. Through books and stories, she found anchors of hope. Through imagination, movement, and visualization, she instinctively propelled herself forward. Long before she had language for them, these tools kept her hopeful, resilient, and beautifully childlike in a world that offered her very little safety.

YOUR TURN

Now, take a moment to read the description of each principle, and then fill out your own personal *Mindset In Motion Method*™ chart using the grid below.

GOAL: What is your goal or dream? What have you wanted to achieve but just haven't put pen to paper and written it down? Are you self-sabotaging? What is the reason why you have not written down your goal or goals? Are you allowing your limiting beliefs to control your desire and stall any action? Take the first step here, write out one goal, and later write out other goals or dreams using the Mindset In Motion Method™ grid. Share it with a friend, family member, community, book club, or other networking group.

BELIEVE: Do you believe you can? If you have a goal or a dream you must believe it will happen. Engrave it in writing. Say the words aloud, or to yourself, even if you are not quite sure how it will happen. Believe. Always speak in the affirmative when you talk about your goals to yourself or another person.

INTERNALIZE: Align your heart and your head to believe and feel you can. Reinforce your mindset to act as though the goal is already achieved. In this step, you will commit through your gratitude practice, meditation, visualization, and journaling to integrate your emotions into creating a connection between what you feel in your heart and know in your head. Speak in terms of the goal achieved rather than one that has not yet been realized.

SHARE: Share your goals and actions with supportive friends, family, colleagues, or partners. It is important to share with supportive people who will support you to achieve your goal.

ACTIVATE: Here's where the hard work comes in. What are you going to do to make it happen? Do you need to find a support system, a community, a mentor, a coach, a therapist, or an advisor? Do you need to take classes or implement a daily and weekly practice schedule? Here is where I say, you are either all in, or you are out! Get into motion, take action, move forward, and look to your goal as achieved!

Make a copy of this page, print multiple copies and outline each goal using the Mindset In Motion Method. It works! A copy is also available at the end of this book.

<u>We Must Know Where We Are Going In Order to Arrive</u>

fdYou don't hop in your car without knowing where you are going. You have a destination in mind. Just as your dream should act as your compass, giving direction and igniting passion for what is possible. Every goal starts with a strong foundation on which to build achievement, and that foundation begins with a vision. While dreaming, journaling, or contemplating your next big goal, allow yourself the space, time, and permission to find clarity, and to dream big, without limits.

Mindset In Motion, principle number two, outlines how believing in yourself is key to achieving your goal. Belief is the fuel behind action. To achieve a goal, you must believe in your ability, even before the results appear. Your

	YOUR GOAL
GOAL	
BELIEVE	
INTERNALIZE	
SHARE	
ACTIVATE	

mindset creates momentum, cultivating confidence and trust in yourself to move forward.

Principle number three is to internalize. Goals stick when they're woven into your daily life and self-identity. When we create a positive daily routine and cultivate good habits, this is when our mind begins internalizing our beliefs. Practicing mental toughness, discipline, and consistency to align your thoughts, habits, and choices with the outcome you want.

Sharing your goal with supportive people is paramount. Do **NOT** share your goals with people who might not support you or may be envious or jealous of your ambition. While no great goal is achieved alone, you should find supportive people with whom you can share your goals and aspirations. **Share your intentions with supportive family members, peers, mentors, coaches and other supportive people** who will encourage and hold you accountable. Positive energy and collaboration expand your capacity to achieve. Good Ideas often occur when engaging in this sort of conversation. One of the reasons I enjoy hosting my podcast, *Mastering the Art of Success*, is the positive collaborative nature, as we share ideas and find that spark of inspiration that propels us to act and implement what we learn from each other in our own business.

The four preceding principles of the Mindset in Motion Method lead up to the most important step: Activate. This is where the hard work comes into play. Action transforms ideas into reality. Even an imperfect action is better than waiting for perfection. The activation stage is about taking consistent steps, overcoming fear, and maintaining resilience when challenges arise. It's about putting in the work, seeking mentorship, hiring a coach, showing up consistently, or finding the right program or course, while surrounding yourself with supportive people.

"Success is never accidental. It's the natural outcome of clear goals, belief, internal alignment, and bold action. Achievement isn't the finish line — it's the person you become in the process."

You should embrace the journey, the lessons, those where you fall flat, and those lessons you conquer, and celebrate milestones and use each win as fuel for future goals. The catalyst for change and for growth can be found in forward thinking and a positive mindset. If you fall, dust yourself off and get back out there. I do not believe in no. I do not believe in impossibility. I believe that "no" is not an option and opportunities are abundant. Every day is greeted with the notion that anything is possible, and I ask myself, "What exciting thing will happen today? I am always on the lookout for opportunities and signs, however small or large, by keeping an open mind and an eye out.

To achieve a goal, the *Mindset in Motion Method*^{TM} shows that you must dream it, believe it, embody it, share it, and take bold action. With this cycle, achievement becomes not just a possibility but an inevitable outcome. One thing is certain: in order to take action, you must plan, prepare, and execute, as we will break down in the next chapter. So get comfortable, and let's move.

Here's a quick cheat sheet to keep on hand when you are seeking to conquer another goal. Pull out your journal or use the pages in this playbook to fill with your own thoughts and answers.

Aligned Action Framework. Pre-Game: Preparation

Before stepping onto the field of action, set yourself up for success.

- **Clarify the Vision**: What do you really want? Picture your desired outcome.

- **Align Your Why**: Why does this matter to you? Connect it to your values.

- **Check Beliefs & Mindset**: Replace limiting thoughts with empowering ones.

Pre-Game is about setting the mental tone. Like an athlete visualizing a win, you're establishing clarity and belief before play begins.

The Game: Taking the Field | This is where mindset meets motion.

- **Define Inspired Actions**: Choose 1–3 actions that feel natural, exciting, and purposeful.

- **Prioritize Flow Over Force**: Notice your energy, lean into actions that energize, not drain.

- **Take the Step & Reflect**: Act, then pause. Did this bring you closer to your vision? Adjust as needed.

During the game, consistency beats intensity. Small aligned moves stack up into momentum.

Post-Game: Reflection and Momentum

Every game ends with a review. This is how progress sticks.

- **Repeat & Build Momentum**: Keep layering aligned steps daily/weekly.

- **Celebrate Small Wins**: Anchor confidence in your growth.

- **Realign**: If something feels off, reset your plan without judgment.

Post-game ensures sustainability. Reflection keeps you in alignment with your evolving goals.

Quick Daily Check-In Questions

- Does this action align with my vision?

- Does it honor my values and energy?

- Will this bring me closer to my desired outcome?

Coach's Note: Just like an athlete returns to fundamentals, you can revisit this framework whenever you feel stuck or misaligned. The game is not won in one play, it's won in the consistent, aligned steps you take over time.

ACTIVITY: Share to Activate

GOAL | Write It Out

Identify one dream or intention that matters deeply to you. It can be personal, professional, or spiritual, but choose something that feels meaningful and true to where you are right now.

____

____

ACTION | Move Forward

1. Write your goal in one clear sentence beginning with _"I am ready to…"_ or _"I am creating…"_

____

____

Example: I am ready to launch my new brand that inspires women to live with intention and confidence.

2. Share it out loud with someone you trust, on social media, or even by recording a voice note for yourself.

____

____

3. Notice how it feels to speak your dream. Does your energy expand? Do you feel a sense of

commitment, excitement, or even fear? All are signs that you've moved closer to activation.

<u>CONNECT | Who Can Help Me?</u>

Reach out to a friend, mentor, or supportive group who aligns with your vision. Share your goal with them and invite gentle accountability. Ask them to check in on your progress, or better yet, to share one of their own goals with you. *When we share our goals, we multiply our momentum. What was once private becomes powerful.*

Reflection Journal Prompts

Take a few quiet minutes to reflect and write:

1. How did it feel to speak my goal out loud?

   ____

2. What emotions surfaced—excitement, fear, relief, or empowerment?

   ____

3. Who did I share my goal with, and how did they respond?

   ____

4. What new opportunities, insights, or support have shown up since I shared it?

   ____

   ____

5. How can I continue to stay accountable to myself and others as I move forward?

   ____

   ____

Note To Self:

Sharing isn't about seeking approval, it's about affirming alignment. Every time you share your dream, you strengthen your belief in it.

PART 2

The Game

Chapter 7

The Game Mindset

"To be a champ, you have to believe in yourself when no one else will." — Sugar Ray Robinson

Early in my career, I attended a Tony Robbins seminar with my real estate colleagues, one of the exercises involved breaking a wooden board with a karate chop. At first, I was skeptical, how could I possibly do this? Yet, with focus and determination, I shattered the board in two with my bare hand. That piece of wood remains a symbol of what's possible when we **challenge our mental barriers**.

Tony taught me that **belief is the foundation for action**. If you believe you can do something, you'll find a way. If you don't, you'll stop before you've even started.

"Whatever you hold in your mind will tend to occur in your life. If you want to change your reality, start by changing your mindset." Anonymous

Once you've decided to take action and you've committed to activating, your goal is now within reach. With both feet firmly on the court, on the playfield, or in the boardroom, you are now in the game. It is time to commit. Once you're in the midst of a dive, there is no turning back. You have taken the first step. You've propelled yourself off the diving board, into the swimming pool, and into the game, and now you must proceed. As you work through the five steps of the Mindset in Motion Method, you start with one mindset. In the beginning, when you are establishing your goal and working on the mindset to believe and internalize your goal, that in itself is one particular mindset, the mindset of preparation. You may even need to convince or brainwash yourself as you work towards the goal and into the activation phase.

The Evolving Mindset: From Preparation to Activation

As you move through the five steps of the *Mindset in Motion Method*, you begin with one mindset, but it doesn't end there. In the beginning, when you're setting your intention and clarifying your goal, you're entering the **Mindset of Preparation**. This is where everything begins. It's the stage of aligning your thoughts, beliefs, and emotions with what you desire, even before it's visible.

At first, you may need to *convince yourself*, to train, reprogram, or even gently **"brainwash"** your mind to believe in what is possible. This is the mental conditioning stage, much like an athlete preparing before a big game or a performer before stepping onto the stage. The visualization of success. You rehearse it mentally. You repeat affirmations, gather inspiration, and prepare yourself emotionally to step into the next version of you. This preparatory mindset is powerful, it builds the foundation of belief. Without it, activation cannot occur.

You are essentially telling your mind, *"This is who I am becoming."* The more you practice believing, the more your subconscious begins to accept it as truth. That's when the shift begins to take hold.

As you continue through the stages, **Believe**, **Internalize**, **Share**, and **Activate,** your mindset evolves. Each phase demands a new level of trust, courage, and embodiment. What once required effort to believe eventually becomes natural. You no longer have to convince yourself; you simply *know*.

By the time you reach activation, your mindset has transformed entirely. What began as mental preparation has become a lived reality. You've moved from imagining the goal to *becoming* the person who embodies it. That is the art and motion of mindset, it's never stagnant; it grows, expands, and evolves as you do.

"Mindset is not a moment, it's a motion. Each phase prepares you for the next version of yourself."

Reflect & Realign

1. What mindset am I currently in; preparation, belief, internalization, sharing, or activation?

2. What thoughts, habits, or beliefs do I need to reprogram to step into my next phase?

3. How can I mentally and emotionally prepare myself to embody the person I am becoming?

A mindset that says, I am ready to go. I am focused and working to make it happen. At this point, you are in activation mode. Next, you need to embrace everything you have and activate it. This is where the hard work comes into play. It's the period in which you ask for help, seek mentors, listen to your coach, listen to your therapist, educate yourself, and surround yourself with supportive people, a strong team, and/or a support group. It takes a village!

The danger of not having the right mindset, or not being "all in," is that you might end up on the bench, may not get the promotion, may lose friends due to depression, or not act as you should by reaching out for help, even hanging out with the wrong people who are not supportive and would rather see you sit on the bench alongside them. You are responsible for your own mindset, not the person next to you. So don't allow a negative, self-deprecating mindset of a teammate or colleague to bring you down.

The activation mindset is the phase where we continually push through to do our best and to win. The anatomy of someone who has a winning mindset will be on the lookout for opportunities and will never look back.

"Don't look back, you are not going that way."

The Lock-In Method

The first thing I do when I am working on any difficult task, project, or goal is to **Lock In**. The Lock In Method^{TM} is a tool to help you focus and enter that flow state by eliminating all distractions. Let's take running, for example. When I run, I do not want to focus on the difficulty of the run, or how boring it can be, so I address this by blocking out any distractions, including my own thoughts. I put my headphones on and tune into my favorites music. I prefer headphones to earbuds, as they cover my ears entirely and allow me to focus more fully. I also use them when I podcast. If I do not lock in, I can be easily distracted. By *locking in,* I become single-minded and laser-focused when I am working to accomplish something important. Using the Lock In Method will eventually put you into that flow state where everything else not important to the task at hand is eliminated.

You must be focused and crystal clear on your goal, winning the game or excelling at your big presentation or meeting. Visualization is a helpful technique to follow. Take the time to sit quietly and walk yourself through the steps, in your mind, of whatever it is you are trying to accomplish. Just like an athlete does before a game.

Here's a **simple 5-step "Lock-In Ritual"** you can use before work or a game. It's short, repeatable, and trains your mind and body to know it's time to focus.

The Lock-In Ritual

1. **Clear and Set** (2 minutes)

- Write down the top 1–3 priorities you want to accomplish.

- Remove or silence distractions (phone on do-not-disturb, tabs closed; even better yet is to put your phone in another room entirely).

2. **Reset Breath** (1 minute)

- Inhale through the nose for 4 seconds.

- Hold for 4 seconds.

- Exhale slowly for 8 seconds.
  Repeat 3 cycles to center your mind.

3. **Anchor Cue** (30 seconds)

- Use a consistent trigger, like putting on headphones, lighting a candle, or saying "I'm locked in" out loud. This becomes your mental switch.

4. **Micro-Move** (1–2 minutes)

- Do a quick body action: a stretch, push-ups, or shaking out your arms and shoulders. This signals energy and readiness.

5. **Launch with Focus** (immediately)

- Start with the most important or challenging task.

- Use a focus timer (e.g., 45 minutes on, 5 minutes off).

Whether I run in my neighborhood or am running in a race, I always LOCK IN by putting on my headphones so I can be completely focused on running and limit any distractions. I prefer to focus solely on the music and not my to-do list. At other times, I use the music to inspire a solution to a problem, work through a difficult conversation I need to have, or explore a project I am working on. The music I choose is key to the activity or mindset I am seeking during that run or race. When I am running in a race, I choose an upbeat playlist to keep me pumped up and moving along. When seeking inspiration on a project, I opt for calmer music. Either way, I am locked in. In less than a mile, I enter that flow state. I cannot enter that flow state without first locking in to alleviate as many distractions as possible. This includes cutting out the environmental noise and nearby chatter, as well as the voices in my head. Be sure to pay attention and be careful when running in a bustling city filled with cars. You do not want to be so locked in that you do not hear a car or bike headed your way. Running on a path, trail, or track is your safest option. Even when I'm hosting my podcast, I must lock in. Wearing headphones blocks out nearby noises and keeps my attention sharp, focused, and completely engaged with my guest. From the moment the opening music plays, I welcome my viewers, and introduce my guest, it is at this point I am totally locked in.

I use the lock-in strategy when I am working, even if I'm the only one in the room. It's similar to closing the door to eliminate distractions in order to make it easier to accomplish what needs to be done. In this case, I do not listen to music; I simply use the headphones as a mechanism to lock in and block out all noise. I don't want to hear other people's conversations and phones ringing when I am serious about completing what it is I am trying to do.

A basketball player at the free throw line, with a stadium full of people yelling, screaming, and even cheering him on, needs to practice being *in the zone*. This is a crucial time for a player to be locked in. Basketball players must train themselves to block out the chatter in order to lock in and make the shot.

How can you do it in your life? How do you cut the noise? The chatter? The negative voices? I was listening to a TED Talk, where a monk was talking about distractions and how we all practice being distracted every day, but we do not practice concentration or stillness. Growing up, we are told to sit still, concentrate, and get our homework done, but we were not taught how to concentrate. Nowadays, we're so distracted. We're practicing distraction most of our lives. Give the *lock-in method* a try and see how it works for you.

Now that you are in the game, commit to moving forward, and work to eliminate distractions so you can focus. The next step is to be on the lookout for opportunities that come your way.

Being Open to Magic

"Opportunities are the stepping stones to success, while possibilities are the fuel that keeps your ambition alive."

I refer to it as *being open to magic*. Keep your mind sharp, and listen to what people are saying or doing. Watch, listen, learn, and be present, or you might just miss the opportunity.

I was at a casual mixer event, and we were all sitting around chatting. The conversation got a little silly, but I was still listening despite not being very interested in what was being said. We may not always enjoy the chatter, but I was there to build relationships. Staying positive and engaging from time to time, I waited it out. At one point, a colleague mentioned something of interest. I took that information to heart, and the next day, I started a real estate marketing campaign. I was inspired to act based on a brief sound bite she shared. That is the kind of spark or magic we are looking for. We never know when or where inspiration or opportunity will strike, opening a new door before us. Another takeaway is to keep an open mind, don't judge, and stay present. If I had not remained in the game and been present in the conversation, I would have missed out on that little gold nugget. It's a small reminder of the importance of a positive mindset vs a negative mindset and remaining present.

Where do you find opportunities? Every day, I am on the lookout for opportunities and gold nuggets. I never know where an opportunity might be lurking. Maybe it is in a conversation or in something I read or heard on MasterClass, Blinkist, the internet, Instagram, or LinkedIn.

One afternoon, my husband offered to host our open house, so I stayed in and started scrolling on Instagram. This one guy kept popping up in my feed. I did a deeper dive into what he was sharing and learned it was about a TEDx course. I listened to the webinar and thought maybe that was my next big thing. Each year, I pick a goal outside of real estate. One year, it was to run a half-marathon, but I signed up for a full marathon instead. Over four years, I wrote four books, not all planned. Each was an opportunity that came my way. A few years in a row, I attended the gifting suites in LA for the Emmys and Oscars; curated events where vendors showcase their product, service or brand to attending celebrities. The celebrities take the time to learn about you and your product and pose for photos. It's a win-win. Everyone gains publicity; it's a fun day, yet a bit exhausting, too. And the year after running the marathon, I launched my podcast, "*Mastering the Art of Real Estate,*" which I rebranded later to "*Mastering the Art of Success*" in order to engage entrepreneurs in all fields.

The TEDx was to be this year's big goal. I started the program, just like that. Adam had not been gone from the house for more than an hour before I discovered my next big thing. I opened Module I and started the program, listening to the coaches and doing the assignments. As I was working and writing to clarify my topic, I realized I had many topics I wanted to share - I asked myself, how was I going to choose just one? How was I going to shorten the right one to just 15 minutes? Which topic would be most interesting to the audience, yet which topic could I speak on effortlessly and effectively while remaining passionate about my chosen topic?

What I realized in that moment was that I really needed to write a book in other to find clarity on my topic. And so it happened. I put down the TEDx materials, opened up a Google Docs tab, and started moving my notes from the course into my newly created Book tab. From there, my new project took flight. While Adam slept, I agonized. By the next morning, when he awoke, I shouted, "I think I have it!" And with that, I was inspired to write another book. Previously, I had vocalized that I had no intention of writing another book. Needless to say, never say never.

Embarking on the journey to write a book is no easy feat. It takes time, a lot of time, patience, concentration, and focus. But my head had a mind of its own, and I could not stop the boulder from rolling down the hill. I was, in fact, in motion and in the game.

The Following 8 Pillars Provide You With A Strong Foundation:

1. **Be on the lookout for magic.** You never know when an opportunity will present itself.

I received an email about an event at the Beverly Hills Chamber. I had been a member years prior but was still receiving invitations. I asked a girlfriend to attend with me. I believe, "nothing ventured, nothing gained," and I was coming into town, so the timing was perfect. I always like to make an effort to meet new people, as you never know what will happen, as it always does.

I was sitting in the meeting contemplating whether or not to join the group. I decided that I would not join as I wasn't coming to LA as often as I had, so I would miss more meetings than I could make. As I made up my mind, I continued listening to the presenter. At this point, I was in the process of writing my book and needed help to finalize it. I was about to sign with a ghostwriter in New York but was reluctant to give my book away for someone else to edit or even add words or contribute their own thoughts and ideas. That didn't feel right. My style is more hands-on. In the meeting, one of the members whom they were showing on the screen identified her profession as a book coach. The presenter was teaching the group how to use Canva. So the member on the screen was simply a placeholder. What transpired was anything but a placeholder. The presenter moved to the next example, the next slide. I was bummed I missed the opportunity to take down the person's information. By a stroke of luck, the speaker scrolled back. I pulled out my phone and snapped a photo.

At that point, I started looking around the room for this person. the networking portion of the meeting, and before everyone stood up and blocked my view, I panned the room. I spotted her. I ran over, trying not to knock down the other members, and sat down next to her and introduced myself. She could not have been nicer and told me her name was Ellie. I told her where I was in my book and asked her how she worked. We set up a meeting for the next day. Within moments of meeting her, I knew she was the right person to help and guide me. Unlike a ghostwriter, Ellie meets with you one-to-one and works with you by asking questions and taking notes. I knew right away it would align with my style. I did not want anyone else's words or interpretations to fill my pages. Yes, I am a bit of a control freak, a passionate one, but very rigid when it comes to my thoughts and words.

> **"What you encounter in the world is a prompt for the next thing."**

When we put out in the universe what we are seeking, we are heard. Be ready when luck or perhaps serendipity presents itself. **I see the world as a big conversation, and I want to be a part of it.** Keep your eyes and ears open.

1. **Look for silver linings.** At work, as in life, we experience ups and downs, both good and bad days. Even in the fog and rain, the sun will eventually shine.

There are opportunities everywhere, even during a global pandemic when it doesn't seem like it. No doubt COVID was horrendous for many people; however, some positive outcomes did come from being locked down. Many had the opportunity to spend time with their family. Many of us learned to work differently, and many discovered hobbies to keep themselves busy. Whether on the sports field, in the office, or in your personal life, keep an open mind and an eye out for those silver linings. Inevitably, we will incur less than desirable experiences, but with the bad, good things eventually take rise. You might have been going in one direction, but something happened that pointed you in a new direction. Keep a lookout for signs. Similar to my meeting with Ellie. I was headed in one direction, to work with the New York ghostwriter, when Ellie seemed to magically appear the very next day here in LA.

2. **Get Help When You Need It.** Don't try to do it all on your own. Look to mentors and coaches. If you don't have a mentor or coach I highly recommend you align yourself with one or both. What you will learn will be invaluable to your

growth and success. Your coaches can be people you know, they can be podcasters or come from online courses. The internet, AI, and YouTube are filled with a wide range of professional and inspirational experts, healers, motivational speakers, self-help and self-improvement gurus, therapists, wellness experts, entrepreneurs, and more, whom you can learn from.

3. **Be Vulnerable.** Over 25 years ago, photographer Quentin Bacon told me I reminded him of Brene Brown. At the time, I hadn't yet discovered her work. But her teachings on vulnerability and courage have profoundly shaped my approach to coaching. Being vulnerable doesn't mean being weak, it means being honest with yourself and others. It's about acknowledging fears and pushing through them.

"Vulnerability is not winning or losing; it's having the courage to show up when you can't control the outcome."

4. **Be a Team Player.** Life is not a solo sport. Being a team player is important in many aspects of life. Be coachsuable when it is time for you to listen and be coached. Whether you are the player, the employee, or the mentee, there comes a time when you must listen and take advantage of opportunities and expertise provided by your coach or mentor. At the same time, you should lift up your teammates, your family, your office, and your community.

My son, 24 at the time, was working as an intern at a commercial real estate firm. He was surrounded by other interns, all from Ivy League colleges. We were discussing what he was doing at the internship and what he was learning. I was pleasantly surprised when he told me, *"I always go in early, and I'm always the last one out."* I thought that was brilliant. For someone doing his first internship and not having any real work experience, it made me proud. His years of playing lacrosse, football, and other sports had given him an instinctive edge: show up, stay committed, and push yourself to go further than the next person. Sports had taught him discipline, endurance, and the value of being a dependable teammate. And it showed up in the workplace, allowing him to stand out without saying a word.

In that moment, I realized that while his peers may have had more prestigious degrees, his greatest advantage came from his mindset. It wasn't about the school typed on his résumé, but the character he carried into the room, a lesson that applies not just in careers, but in life.

5. **Be Accountable.** When we hold ourselves accountable, or have someone to do it for us, we are far more likely to follow through.

"Accountability is the glue that ties commitment to results."—Bob Proctor

6. **No Is Not An Option.** Words I live by, the foundation of every goal I've ever decided to conquer. I've been sharing that phrase with my children and everyone who crosses my path: my kids' friends, those who ask how I achieve what I

have, my mentees, coaching clients, other agents, and anyone in my Debbi Vortex.

7. **Just Do It.** Don't overthink. Don't stagnate; execute. Not finishing is simply not an option. We must commit at the start to see it through. "No is not an option" and "**Every breakthrough in your life begins with one decision: yes.**" encapsulates a powerful philosophy centered around the importance of embracing opportunities and challenges.

At its core, the mantra emphasizes the idea that saying "no" can often close doors to potential growth, success, and experiences. By adopting a mindset that views "yes" as an essential gateway, we're encouraged to step outside of our comfort zones and tackle new ventures, even when it seems daunting.

Opportunities often lie beyond initial reluctance or fear. When you **just do it**, you approach life proactively. You embrace possibilities that can lead to unforeseen rewards, both personally and professionally. **This mindset fosters resilience, creativity, and openness to change, which are crucial traits for navigating life's complexities.**

In essence, my mantra serves as a reminder that fortune favors the bold. By choosing to say "yes," we may discover new paths, forge valuable connections, and unlock our full potential, ultimately leading to a more fulfilling and enriched life.

Over the years, I can cite many wins by simply embracing these words. My first book, *Contained Beauty, Photographs, Reflections, and Swimming Pools,* catapulted into reality due to a chance meeting. My journey is a testament to the power of resilience and seizing opportunities. It all began one fateful evening when I reluctantly attended a party, feeling out of sorts and questioning my decision to go. Little did I know that my presence at this gathering would change my life forever, propelling me forward and allowing me to walk through doors previously unknown.

Our daughter had just returned from her first semester away at college, and I was beyond excited to see her. Adam and I arrived late, as we wanted to give our daughter a big welcome home hug. The very first person I saw upon arrival was Rob Bond, a publisher whom I did not know personally. He was the husband of my charity colleague and friend. But I did not know him. However, just as I preach and teach, when you see an opportunity, you must take it. I wasn't feeling particularly confident, but I pushed myself and forged ahead. That little voice in my head said, "It would not be smart of you to let this opportunity go." He was literally right in front of me, and because we were late, the crowd had thinned. It was as if I manifested this meeting. Just a short time before this chance meeting, I had begun internalizing the fact that I was, in fact, going to bring my coffee table book to life. And like magic, there he stood.

Rob, a very tall, thin man who seemed to rise above everyone else in the room. I mustered up the courage and walked right up to him, introduced myself, and with that, he disarmed any nerves I had, saying he knew who I was and that his wife thought highly of me. I was so relieved our conversation came so naturally. I asked if he might sit down with me sometime to discuss an idea I had for a book. He replied without hesitation and suggested I phone him after the holidays. I left that night with excitement and the knowledge that the possibility of this book happening would have some direction. I was in motion. The next day, I started detailing an exact outline down to the color of the interior of the first and last pages. I left nothing to chance. I also sent Rob a thank-you note and said I would reach out in January. We met, and the rest is history.

I realized that by embracing the mindset "No Is Not An Option" and Nike's, "Just Do It", I could overcome any obstacle by simply being alert, open to opportunities, and aware of people who are placed in front of us at any given time. Furthermore, you need to seize the moment and ask. No one is a mind reader.

My story did not end with the publication of the first book. It only serves as a reminder to be open to new experiences, to push past self-doubt, and to recognize that opportunities can arise in the most unexpected places. My journey is a celebration of creativity, determination, and the belief that embracing possibilities can lead to extraordinary outcomes. In the years that followed, I have continued to create, inspire, and empower others to pursue their passions, always holding onto the mantra that **every "no" can lead to a resounding "yes!"**

Look forward, never back. You are not going that way.

When I coach and mentor, it's most often the same: the client, mentee, or student questions and doesn't simply believe what I am sharing with them. When I was working under my mentors, I took every opportunity to listen, digest, and implement. Sure, I had questions, but I did not debate or second-guess them. I believe that is why I rose to the top so quickly.

8. **Identify Your Mentor.** Identify the right mentor and follow their lead. It took years to get where they are today, so why doubt their strategy? If they are not the right person, then move on. If they are, and you surely have witnessed their success, or why did you choose them in the first place? Be appreciative, follow their lead, and don't waste their time. Beyond that, reciprocate, follow through, and thank them for their time and expertise.

9. **'No Excuses'** In coaching, this is my most used phrase followed closely by "No *is not an option.*"

You can't embrace a positive mindset while making excuses. There is always a way. You must move forward, seek answers, ask for help, and refuse to give up. Whatever you are seeking to do, if you work with a positive mindset, you will find an answer, a course, a person, or a professional to guide you from Point A to Point B. Don't give up or come up with excuses. Either work to find an answer, conquer a goal, overcome a challenge, or work against yourself. It's up to you.

Need to find motivation to get yourself in motion? Give the 5-Second Rule a try. In recent years, Mel Robbins has become a significant influencer. Her 5-Second Rule, counting backward from five to overcome hesitation, is a simple but powerful tool.

"If you have an impulse to act on a goal, you must physically move within five seconds, or your brain will kill it." —Mel Robbins

In this chapter, we discussed the Lock-In Method and how this strategy gives us an edge. By blocking out the noise, it gives us the opportunity to focus on the task at hand, whether going for a run, preparing for a big speech, gearing up for a race, or heading into an important game. When we lock in and quiet the noises around us, it allows us to better concentrate and become completely absorbed and immersed in our goal.

We also reviewed the key elements of the athlete's mindset while in the game so that you can better see the opportunities that are available to you.

Which of these elements most resonated?

____

____

Which comes easily?

____

____

Which can you implement more thoughtfully?

____

____

How are you going to LOCK IN and position yourself with the right mindset to propel forward and into action? Where can you utilize the Lock-In Method to help you achieve your goals?

Remember,

"Your mindset dictates your actions."

GOALS | Write It Out

- When can I use the Lock-In Method to focus? There are many ways I can benefit from the lock-in method to achieve my goals.

____

____

ACTION | Move Forward

- Where can I work best to lock in and focus on what I am trying to accomplish?

____

____

CONNECT | Who Can Help Me?

- Who can support me in my need for private time? Do I need to ask for space? Do I need to alert someone that I will be taking this time? Family members, colleagues, spouses, significant others, children? Tip: Set a timer to keep you on task while allowing time for breaks.

____

____

Chapter 8

Mindset vs. Attitude, Leading with Positivity and a Winning Attitude

"You do not need to roar like a lion to rule the jungle." –Debbi DiMaggio

I previously told you the story of how my son sought to stand out and be noticed by his boss. He was always the first to arrive in the morning and always the last to leave. This quiet gesture demonstrates how we can vary our efforts to be noticed. Our action does not have to be loud. We do not have to shout or overshadow a colleague or team member. And in that silence is where the power lies. Our winning attitude says, *I am present, I care, and I mean business.*

What is the difference between mindset and attitude? Our mindset is reserved for us; it is how we choose to maneuver each day. Will I greet the day and its multiple tasks with a positive or negative mindset? It is personal. Mindset is positioning yourself strategically in order to follow through with whatever it is you need to do. Refer back to your morning routine; that is an excellent way to set yourself up for a successful day and a positive mindset.

Our attitude, on the other hand, affects others. It is not reserved just for us. While mindset is personal, attitude touches those around us. In order to affect others with our positive attitude, we must utilize tools and strategies to help us remain in the right mindset, being proactive, positive, and present, while wanting the team, our business partners, and our colleagues to succeed.

We do not usually say, "Jack has a positive mindset." That is his personal disposition, but we do say, "Jack has a positive attitude" or "Jack has a negative attitude." Our attitude is noticed by others, and those around us can be directly affected by our mood and mindset. One's attitude is like a hand, either patting you gently on the back or knocking you down with one swift blow. It's about how you affect people, which can be negative or positive. When you witness someone walking down the street who has a negative attitude, your instinct is to stay clear of that person. And if the person is smiling, you might smile back or even say hello.

In business, for example, when someone has a bad attitude, no one wants to be around that person. Your colleagues will not be interested in asking you out to lunch, nor in participating in any group activity, whether social or business-related. Your colleagues will tolerate you as they must and as is needed in an office, but guaranteed they will not extend themselves to you. If you do not have a positive attitude and are not proactive or taking initiative, ownership, or demonstrating consistent growth, your boss will have little reason to offer you new opportunities.

Without a positive, can-do attitude and mindset, bosses, coaches, and leaders are far less inclined to invest their time or resources into your advancement. Growth opportunities don't just appear, they are unlocked. And those doors often stay closed when you don't show the initiative, energy, or vision that makes a leader want to invest in you.

Think about it this way: your boss has countless responsibilities and limited time. They are scanning their team for individuals who not only perform well but also inspire confidence. If you show up day after day doing only what's asked, without stretching further, leading, or bringing fresh ideas with a positive mindset and attitude, your boss will not feel compelled to create new pathways for you.

Keep in mind that others are always watching and assessing your attitude. It's instinctive; it's what we do when we are in the presence of another. How many times have you skirted around a person because you knew they usually had something negative to say, either complaining about work, their life, or the state of the economy? No one wants to be around someone who consistently has a negative attitude. We all endure our own personal trials and tribulations, good and bad days, but we don't need to share our negative thoughts all the time. Would you want to be around you if that were your demeanor all of the time?

"You are the average of the five people you spend the most time with." — Jim Rohn

I take this quote to heart and repeat it to myself often as a reminder to check in. Who are the five people you spend the most time with?

The idea behind it is that your mindset, habits, and ultimately your success are strongly influenced by the people you surround yourself with. Their attitudes, values, and behaviors will either lift you or hold you back.

- **Energy and mindset**: Spend time with positive, motivated people, and their energy will influence you.

- **Habits and standards**: The group you associate with often sets the standard for what you consider "normal" in terms of work ethic, lifestyle, and ambitions.

- **Growth and success**: Surrounding yourself with people who inspire and challenge you encourages personal and professional growth.

Exercise: Take a moment to jot down your thoughts.

1. List famous or influential people you admire. They can be celebrities, entrepreneurs, CEOs, athletes, or people you know of distantly but not yet personally.

---

2. Make a list of famous, known, or influential people whom you would NOT like to be around, who exemplify poor behavior and a negative attitude?

---

3. Make a list of people you need to remove from your life.

---

4. Make a list of people you know and admire who you would like to hang out with and have in your *Top 5* circle.

Who can you drop and who can you add to your list to improve your personal and professional growth? Each morning, as part of your daily routine, glance at the list and see if you can make progress towards list Number 4.

When I'm deciding who to invite to collaborate on a project or help lead one of our events, there are a handful of people who immediately come to mind. They're dependable, represent the brand well, and always come prepared. Afterward, they follow up with thoughtful insights and feedback about how things went, which helps us continually improve. For a while, there was another person on that list. But over time, I realized they no longer belonged there. Whenever I tried to ask follow-up questions, the response was defensive, negative or simply no response at all. Communication became inconsistent, marked by delayed responses, excuses, and even a missed appointment.

What stood out most wasn't the occasional mistake, we all make those. It was the attitude. Instead of recognizing the opportunity to contribute and collaborate, their energy suggested they were doing me a favor. That subtle shift in mindset made all the difference. With that kind of energy, I quietly moved away.

Would you continue giving opportunities to someone who treated you that way? Would you stay in a toxic, abusive or even a mediocre friendship or relationship? Most of us wouldn't. In every environment, whether in business, athletics, creative partnerships, or even within our friends and families, people naturally gravitate toward positivity. When we work with people who bring good energy into the room, it elevates everyone around them.

It motivates us to support, recommend, and open doors for them.

A positive attitude is contagious. It's been over a year since I last considered that person for a collaboration, and I don't miss the dynamic at all. Looking back, I realized how much unnecessary tension it created. Sometimes we don't recognize how draining something is until it's no longer part of our day-to-day experience. Is there someone you have experienced this dynamic with in your own life? Is there someone in your life now creating this same tension? Is it time to let go and move on? The lesson is simple. If you carry a negative attitude and expect people to continue inviting you into opportunities or elevating you, think again. Over time, you will quietly be passed over. Colleagues, teammates, leaders, and even family members naturally gravitate toward people who bring optimism, professionalism, and a willingness to contribute. When we are in the presence of positive-minded people, we don't just appreciate them, we root for them. We want to see them succeed, and we're often eager to help them along the way. It is the reason I wrote this book: to help others find their own success. —That's the power of attitude.

Attitude and Ego

You may have had a friend or worked with a colleague whose ego walked in the door even before they did. You know those people. You see them coming and want to run. My friend had a colleague who helped this person build his brand and even asked him to join the team when he was with another firm. His ego got so inflated that he became impossible to tolerate. His colleagues who once supported him, until his attitude became so pompous that they just wanted to run the other way when he walked through the door or his name popped up on their phone. A once demure, kind person allowed his ego to become so inflated that it overshadowed the very qualities that once made him so likable. Don't become that person.

"Anyone can manage pressure. Character is revealed in how you handle power, influence, and opportunity."

Your innate disposition toward others reveals the essence of who you truly are. How do you show up when no one is watching, and there are no consequences for your choices? Do you still lead with kindness and integrity?

One of my favorite quotes:

"Character is revealed in how we treat others when no one is watching."

No matter how good you are at what you do, how famous you are, or how much money you have, a bad attitude can get you blacklisted in your industry. In the acting world, there are many stories of very talented and famous actors who were blacklisted because their attitudes became toxic (Ask ChatGPT or Google, and you will find a list).

The same can be said about real estate agents, agents want to work with other agents who are going to play nice and collaborate for the common goal, which is to serve clients. The expectation is that all players be kind, communicative, and true to both their word and the contract.

Whether in the acting world or in real estate, these communities are intimate circles; rest assured, everyone knows what is going on. If you want the role, or want to win the deal for your client, play nice, embrace a positive attitude, and check your ego at the door. Just as on a sports team, in a family, or in your particular industry, **attitude makes all the difference.**

Have you ever done this? Maybe you had a bad day, and the next day you knew you needed and wanted to start the day with a better and more positive attitude. So you changed it. You told yourself to shape up, and you did. I bet things went much better for you. It may have started a bit phony as you tried to embrace a positive attitude when you weren't yet feeling it. (That is the Believe step in the Mindset in Motion Method—*believe even if you are not yet convinced.*) But once you did, your day brightened, and people approached you as they had not done the day before. Changing your attitude changes your behavior. It is up to you to take personal responsibility and hold yourself accountable.

If you want to be successful, you have to be pleasant. When you have a bad attitude, it's an uphill battle. No one wants to work with a negative, unhappy, or miserable person. Even if you are the perfect person for the role, the job, or the position, rest assured, those in power will go out of their way not to give it to you.

The good news is that you can change your attitude and cultivate an attitude that makes people want to be around you, see you succeed, help you, work with you, and watch you grow. When I coach, I enjoy watching my clients flourish. I am not going to lie, but when they are ready to fly, it's bittersweet, as I miss our time together.

"Being just one percent better every day is compound interest for your body and mind, where every day's gain gets added to yesterday's principal, so that you earn results on your results. Doing something small each day will leave you with more of everything: more strength, more confidence, and more possibilities. Attitude is the difference maker."
– John Maxwell

Here's a list of positive and winning attitudes. These are qualities you will want to embrace to rise to the top and be noticed by those around you who are in a position to elevate and help you in your journey.

- **Kind:** Be pleasant to be around.

- **Contribute:** Ask what or how you can contribute. Be someone who contributes to the conversation, the team, the family, and the group.

- **Fit it in.** Successful people find time. They don't make excuses; they don't say, "I'm too busy." If you want to be seen, you need to say yes. People need to know you are reliable. You will not get very far if you don't show up or complain when you do. I always recommend to newer agents that if they want to be known, they need to show up and be seen. When you are in the office, opportunities arise, and you learn from your colleagues, bosses, and even the staff. The staff most likely knows a little about everything, and getting to know them is invaluable. It's not the CEO you need to call on; it's the executive assistant who keeps her calendar.

- **Say yes.** Say yes to everything that comes your way. It's the person with the positive attitude who always shows up who will win, whether that is a referral or a shot at an opportunity that otherwise would not have come your way.

- **Be a team player.** No one wants to work with someone who believes "it's all about me." A team player shows he cares and demonstrates an earnest desire to help everyone succeed. When you lack that skill, you are easily passed over. Remember to check that ego elsewhere. Don't bring it to the office, a family gathering, or onto the sports field.

I am a member of the networking group BNI, Business Networking International. It has only been a few years, but the lessons I have learned have been invaluable to my coaching and writing. The BNI core values below align perfectly with this chapter. By embracing a positive and winning attitude, we all succeed.

Give First: Focus on providing value, referrals, support, and opportunities to others without expecting immediate returns.

Mutual Benefit: Over time, the goodwill you create builds strong trust and relationships. That trust naturally leads to others giving back, often in greater measure.

Long-Term Mindset: Instead of transactional networking ("What can I get now?"), it emphasizes relationship-building ("How can I help you grow?"). Implement the BNI core values and watch your network open up.

Homework:

To grow your business, build relationships. Draft a networking schedule (in ink) with a <u>minimum</u> of two meetings per week. Meetings can be in person, on Zoom, or on the phone; however, an in-person meeting is much more effective. And be sure to follow up with a note so the person has something tangible to remember you by. Jot down a few people you would like to have meetings with and keep adding to the list. Bonus: Add the names to your CRM or Excel spreadsheet.

____

____

<u>Running on Mindset, Winning with Attitude</u>

When I ran the LA Marathon, I didn't finish on athletic training alone, I finished because of **mindset**. My body screamed to stop, but my mind kept whispering, "*One more step.*" *Keep going.* That inner voice carried me through the miles when I wanted to give up.

But crossing that finish line wasn't just about my internal drive. Along the course, strangers cheered me on, volunteers handed out water with encouragement, and fellow runners gave nods of solidarity. Their **attitude** lifted me higher than my mindset alone could. It reminded me: *mindset gets you moving, but attitude spreads the energy, lifting everyone in your path.*

Mindset: Your Personal Inner Game

Your **mindset** is deeply personal, it's the way you think, the beliefs you carry, and the narrative you repeat to yourself. A growth mindset says, "*I can learn, I can adapt, I can improve.* A fixed mindset says, "*This is just the way I am.*" I am certain you can name a few people you know with a fixed mindset.

"Mindset is the driver. Everything else is the result."

"Mindset is the silent force shaping how you see challenges, seize opportunities, and decide who you become."

<u>Attitude: The Energy You Project</u>

Your **attitude**, on the other hand, is external. It's how your mindset shows up in the world. Your tone, your body language, and the way you treat others, all of these create an atmosphere that either uplifts or weighs down the people around you.

- A **positive attitude** opens doors, builds trust, and inspires collaboration.

- A **negative attitude** shuts people down, drains energy, and blocks possibility.

- An **ego-driven attitude** might impress in the short term but ultimately isolates, creating distance rather than connection.

<u>Why the Distinction Matters</u>

You can have a strong mindset internally, but if your outward attitude is defensive, arrogant, or dismissive, it erases the benefits. People do not feel your private thoughts, they experience your **attitude**. That is why it's essential to align the two: nurture a mindset that fuels you and project an attitude that elevates others.

GOALS | Write It Out

- Recognize the difference between mindset (personal) and attitude (relational).

- Commit to cultivating a positive outlook that fuels resilience internally and builds trust externally.

- Identify triggers where negativity or ego takes over and shift consciously.

____

____

ACTION | Move Forward

1. Begin each morning by setting both a **mindset and intention** (*How do I want to think today?*) and an **attitude of intention** (*How do I want others to experience me today?*).

____

____

2. Keep a journal where you record moments when your attitude influenced a group, positively or negatively. Reflect on the outcome.

____

____

3. The next time you feel ego or negativity rising, pause and ask: *Is this helping me connect or pushing people away?*

____

____

<u>CONNECT | Who Can Help Me?</u>

- Share with a friend, colleague, or coach one way your attitude has impacted a situation.

____

____

- Invite honest feedback: How do you experience me? Do I bring positivity, or do I carry tension into the room?

____

____

- Surround yourself with people who model the kind of attitude you aspire to live daily. Name 3 to 5 positive, supportive people.

____

____

Chapter 9

Discipline

"We must all suffer one of two things: the pain of discipline or the pain of regret and disappointment."
– Jim Rohn

At nearly 60, I accomplished a milestone I was not sure was possible. I set out to do it solely on *mindset* to prove we can adjust our mindset to make things happen. It was a test of endurance, mindset, and **sheer willpower**.

How Did I Do It?

I broke down the preceding months and the day of the race in my head. Before the LA Marathon (January/February 2024), I ran a few 5Ks and 10Ks, took a few SoulCycle classes, and ran a few miles here and there, but never had I run longer than the two half marathons (the first at 19 or 20 years old, the second at 59). What is impressive or crazy, is that I had just started running the 2.5 months preceding the LA Marathon, January and February, and part of March; however, it was very intermittent. It was the morning of December 31st, 2023, when I propelled myself into thought and into motion, and on December 31st, any thought of running a half-marathon, let alone a full marathon, had ever crossed my mind.

When I made the decision to sign up for the marathon, it was not more than one month in advance. Needless to say, I did not leave myself much time to train. But that was not part of this particular journey. This was a test to see if a person could run a marathon with little to no training, on mindset alone. I immersed myself in books about soldiers and the elite Navy SEALs who had achieved incredible feats, not only during training but also during high-risk military operations, thereby conditioning my brain. My training came in the form of disciplining my mind. I read and listened to books and watched YouTube videos. I became a bit obsessed. I also thought about how running 26+ miles might affect my body, legs, feet, shins, knees, and heart, contemplating whether I could physically do it. But I told myself I had no reason to fail.

I hesitated to share my goal. What if I didn't finish? What if I hurt myself, or my legs physically could not perform or complete the duration of the 26.2 miles? But for some reason, it just didn't seem possible not to complete what I set out to do. I knew it was my nature always to look forward, so this line of questioning was unlike me. Normally, when I set an intention, I visualize it, internalize it, speak it into existence, and make it happen. But this time, uncertainty crept in. Still, I pressed forward, *reminding myself that fear has no place in the pursuit of our dreams, while discipline and mindset are paramount to conquering our goals. So I went for it.*

Where there is a will, there is a way. The race itself was grueling, especially around mile 18. Fatigue set in, but so did my inner voice: "*You are not an 'almost.' You finish what you begin.*" That mindset carried me across the finish line while tears came streaming down my cheeks. I guess I even surprised myself that I had finished.

Along the way, I drew inspiration from people who faced challenges far greater than a 26.2-mile race—my grandmother, Stella, who passed away far too young from cancer, and friends battling cancer and multiple sclerosis, whose daily strength reminded me of the power of perseverance and discipline. I chose to dedicate my run to all of them. At that point, it turned the race around. It wasn't *my* race; it was a race for all of those who cannot, whether by physical disability or disease. But I could. I was one of the lucky ones. So I ran on.

This experience reinforced what I've always believed: **success isn't just about talent or training—it's about mindset, commitment, determination, persistence,** and **discipline**. These same principles drive me in every area of life. They are my North Star. Whether running a marathon, moving into a new chapter in life, or pursuing a dream, the key is to believe in yourself, push through doubt, and commit fully to the journey.

> *"Achieving a goal requires clarity of purpose, self-belief, commitment, discipline, determination, and the power of visualization."*

I wrote this affirmation before the marathon to stay focused and motivated. And on March 17, 2024, I crossed the finish line. What is your marathon? It may not be 26.2 miles, but whatever goal you are chasing, know this: You *can* achieve it. Once you set a goal, believe in it, internalize it, and commit to it by sharing that goal with supportive people, and most importantly, put in the work and move forward.

<u>What Is Discipline?</u>

Discipline has many arms, many tentacles. Discipline is more than one thing. Discipline is a compilation of talent, physical stamina, and mental toughness, layered with commitment, mindset, persistence, and determination. If you are an athlete with talent and stamina and are disciplined while in the game and even at practice, do you have the mental fortitude and discipline to keep your personal life in check? How do you manage your mental attitude and ego? Do you practice meditation or do drugs? Will you have discipline when everyone is coming at you from every which way and wants something from you? Will you be able to handle the fame? The attention? Oftentimes, drugs and alcohol prevail. Even suicides result from talent and fame, because the person was unable to handle it.

Discipline can be described in two ways. Discipline in Action and Discipline of the Mind. Discipline in Action is the external form of discipline and what we do consistently in the real world. Take, for instance, our habits and routines. Are you sticking to your exercise routine? Practicing healthy eating? Do you show up on time and follow through? Are you motivated, and do you take action even when you don't feel like it? Do you let discipline carry you on when motivation dips? Are you persistent? Do you stay the course despite setbacks, distractions, and obstacles? Do you choose long-term rewards over short-term pleasures, implementing delayed gratification to finish the project, finish the course, and play hard until the end? Take, for example, an athlete training every morning at 4 AM, regardless of the weather or his mood. This attitude demonstrates discipline in action, as well as the person who arrives early to work, or practices his free throw shot over and over and over again, or the golfer perfecting his golf swing until his palms are blistered.

Discipline Of The Mind is the internal form of discipline, the mastery of thoughts, emotions, and focus. This is the strategy I employed to run the LA Marathon. I hadn't committed to months of conditioning or taken the time to understand the many components of marathon training. I was largely unaware of what it truly demanded, physically, mentally, and nutritionally. When we describe the Discipline of the Mind, four steps come into play.

1. **Mental Control:** Steering your thoughts away from negativity, fear, or distraction. I was conditioning my mind to believe I could do it regardless of what anyone might say to me; thus, I did not share my decision to run the marathon with anyone but my husband. And I did not want to do so until only one week prior to the race. I did not

want other voices in my head distracting me from my mission.

2. **Focus:** Directing your energy toward what matters most instead of scattering it. I focused solely on my own thoughts, audiobooks, and YouTube videos. I immersed myself in learning about how one uses a disciplined mind to achieve their goals. I do believe I was, in fact, brainwashing myself in order to prove it could be done.

3. **Resilience:** Cultivating calm in the face of stress, rejection, or uncertainty. I utilized my morning and evening routines to practice running the race, though only in my mind. I also used my mind to keep myself centered and focused. I did not allow negative thoughts to fill my head. My self-talk was positive before and during the race, like a spirited cheerleader. And I did not allow anyone to get in the way of what I had sought to accomplish.

4. **Mindset Alignment:** Training your mind to believe in your goals, visualize success, and maintain self-belief. As I mentioned, I did not share my plans ahead of time and continued to keep my story to myself even while sitting on the bus heading towards the stadium to the starting line. I was chatting with my seatmate. The young man was sharing his training schedule. I was holding my breath, repeating to myself, 'Please do not ask me how I trained.' I kept peppering him with questions so he could not squeeze in a question of his own. He went on to say he had run across the San Mateo Bridge as one of his last training sessions. I, on the other hand, enjoyed two, maybe three, glasses of wine and a chicken Caesar salad the night before

the race. Not your typical meal, and you now know my training schedule, or lack thereof.

Discipline of the mind guides your focus and strengthens your willpower. A writer overcoming self-doubt and writer's block by training their mind to focus on progress, not perfection, demonstrates discipline of the mind. At the same time, discipline in action and in motion translates that inner strength into consistent habits repeated and compounded over time to achieve results.

Commitment, like persistence, mindset, and determination, is foundational to discipline. Once I was committed to running the race, I found the discipline to execute. But first I had to commit. A **definite chief aim,** as taught by Napoleon Hill, is a single, clearly defined, dominant life purpose that becomes the central focus of your thoughts and actions. It must be specific in what you desire, include a definite time frame for its achievement, outline the value or service you will give in return, and be supported by a practical plan. By making this aim your continuous focus, writing it down, affirming it daily, and aligning all decisions with it, you impress it upon your subconscious mind. Over time, this persistent concentration of thought and energy attracts opportunities, resources, and people, propelling you toward your objective with clarity, precision, and power.

Before a commitment is made, it starts out as a thought, an idea, or the possibility of something one desires to achieve. After the commitment is set in stone, the act or goal becomes "definite," and you do whatever you can to align yourself to achieve that goal. And this is where discipline comes into play.

Let's take real estate, for example. Many people set out to become real estate agents. They spend weeks and months taking the courses, and then they study for the test. While obtaining a test date is oftentimes weeks out, and maybe after one, two, or even three tries, they finally pass. At this juncture, they are excited that they are about to become a licensed agent. Receiving their test results and obtaining the license also takes time. Next, they interview with offices and finally choose an office to join. They pay dues to all the various organizations, order their signs, get their business cards, and take their first training. They still seem totally committed. But once they have completed all of those hurdles and taken a few classes, it is almost as if they get stuck in their tracks. Because now they are licensed but do not have any business. Finding clients takes time and patience.

Although they now have the license, they still have zero experience. What happens more often than not is they host a few open houses, they stop coming into the office, and they eventually disappear. Where do they go? What are they doing? I have no idea. The issue is that they lack the discipline to execute. They have all the tools they need, beyond business cards and signs, they have the backing of their office staff, their broker, and their manager, as well as endless training and mentorship, should they choose to put in the work.

Once you fall off the radar, not only do you lose credibility within your own office, but also with the public. If you are not showing up, how are you going to convince someone to either refer you business or hire you to work with them as their agent? And how do you expect to gain experience, knowledge, and thus skills to build your business? Furthermore, your agent colleagues will not want to work with or collaborate with you if you fail to show up or demonstrate interest and engagement. No one wants to invest time in training and mentoring when there is a lack of interest and the person is not showing up or putting in the hard work day in and day out. Without structure and the discipline to show up, commit to oneself, and put in the hard work, failure is at their doorstep. Oftentimes, agents will end up going back to the job they came from or finding something else to do.

Real estate is not easy, but anything worth doing takes time and effort. Results are only achieved through effort and discipline. There is no shortcut to success. What shows their lack of determination and commitment is when an agent says they are going to do something, followed by either a no-show and/or more excuses. "I am too busy," is the sound of nails on a chalkboard. You can never be too busy for your clients nor your business if you wish to succeed. As a coach, I empower not only Realtors but also entrepreneurs and individuals to conquer their goals, whether launching a business, growing a brand, or pursuing personal success.

I was coaching a friend who was seeking to launch a product. We spent a few months going through all the steps. I was sharing information and providing every step and detail down to who could implement each part of the process, from attorneys, canning companies, and food production companies to branding, trademarking, and licensing. That was the fun part, the easy part. But when it was time to take a test and move to the next stage, she stalled out. We worked together to get her through it, eventually.

I explained that I could teach and guide her, but I couldn't take the test for her. And once the product was created, she would be the one responsible for promoting and selling it, because she is the brand. I sensed early on that once she fully understood how demanding a product launch would be, she might reconsider. In the end, she chose not to move forward. Had she jumped in without understanding the licensing, fees, required courses, regulations, personal liability, time commitment, insurance, trademarking, and everything else involved, she likely would have invested a significant amount of money only to face a major loss, along with unnecessary stress and wasted time.

She came to find out she did not want to put in that kind of effort. She really did not have the time and did not want to make the time needed to make her product a success. She did not want to employ the kind of discipline it would take. Thankfully she learned early on that she was not committed to making it happen. It was a goal of hers, even a passion, but in the end, she was not committed once she discovered how much work it would entail to launch her product, let alone the big unknown of whether or not her product would be a success.

If someone wants to achieve a goal, you can coach them through it. But sometimes, after going through all the steps, they realize they do not have the discipline and fortitude to actually go through with it. Accomplishing one's goals takes time, energy, and putting oneself out there. Simply put, without discipline, the work doesn't get done. However, even when you don't follow through on a specific goal or project, there is still value to be gained. Every experience carries a lesson, and each lesson moves you closer to your true purpose, even if you haven't yet defined it.

Do You Really Have What It Takes?

Talent only gets you so far; discipline gets you the rest of the way.

"You don't have to be the smartest person in the room. You have to be the most disciplined."

Many people have great ideas, start projects, and attempt goals but do not finish because of a lack of discipline. If you wish to achieve a goal, you must commit and implement. When I make a statement that I am going to do something, I'll do everything in my power to make it happen, or I will not say it. I believe in sharing only what I am truly going to do. I have a friend who talks about wanting to do things all the time, but never follows through. Do you have a friend like that? She just talks and talks. It is the 80/20 rule: 20% of people do 80% of the work.

Words of wisdom I would tell my 20-year-old self: "Hang in there, be patient." "Nurture a positive mindset and work at being disciplined." "Don't give up; success takes time." "Keep pushing forward and enjoy the journey." The cool thing is, once you are committed and working with a disciplined mindset, you are in motion, locked in, and ready to go! We use discipline to build habits, which build momentum to push us towards the positive results we are seeking to achieve. And once in motion and repeatedly doing something, it will become a habit, and soon after, discipline is not needed quite as much, because that action becomes routine. When setting out to conquer a goal, you need discipline, a lot of it, and eventually, it is **momentum that propels** you forward.

How Do You Remain Disciplined?

We all have areas in our lives where we are extremely disciplined and have areas in our lives where we have fallen off track. Some of us are committed to eating healthy, adhering to a workout schedule, practicing yoga or meditation, or completing daily tasks. Others do not have the focus or discipline to follow through on an assignment, task, or goal. Building that discipline muscle is first and foremost to developing habits. The more you implement, the easier it becomes to continue. *Discipline, repetition, routine, habit, momentum, repeat.*

When I ran out my front door that cool, crisp morning on December 31st, 2023, my mind was made up. I wasn't thinking much about it. I just started. I simply put on my running shoes and set out on a run and knew that momentum would thrust me forward. I had made up my mind to *just do it.* And in writing this book, once I made up my mind to do it, I shared it, made a commitment to myself, and shared it out loud. This time, I needed some help to push on, whereas in running, I did not want or need any assistance.

I discovered in finishing this book that I needed to figure out how to be more disciplined. I needed to learn how to sit down and focus. It is much easier for me to be in motion. The difficulty lies when I have to be still. Working with two coaches helped me to find the discipline I needed to overcome the obstacles in front of me.

Seeking support to achieve our goals isn't a weakness, it's a strength that successful people consistently embrace. Many high achievers employ multiple coaches to keep them disciplined and on track. When someone is watching, encouraging, and providing guidance, it becomes easier to show up consistently, even on the days you don't feel like it. That accountability begins to shift into self-discipline, and you start building habits that will carry you forward, even when no one is looking. It's okay to get help; actually, it is paramount to continued and long-lasting success. You don't have to do it all alone. You simply need to identify the right, supportive people to assist you with your goals.

Serena Williams, one of the greatest tennis players of all time, has worked with multiple coaches simultaneously. Here are some of the different types of coaches and support professionals she has had throughout her career: Tennis Coach, Strength & Conditioning Coach, Nutritionist, Physiotherapist, Sports Psychologist, Hitting Partner, and Fitness Trainer.

Former Google CEO Eric Schmidt has credited his success to coaching, famously saying, *"Everyone needs a coach." Coaches include:* Executive Coach, Leadership Coach, Public Speaking Coach, Strategy Advisor, Communication Coach, and Negotiation Coach. Oprah has openly shared about using various coaches and mentors throughout her career. Life Coach, Spiritual Coach, Speaking/Media Coach, Business Coach, Health & Wellness Coach, Nutritionist, and a Personal Trainer.

<u>**GOALS | Write It Out**</u>

What are the goals I wish to accomplish?

- Define your definite chief aim.

____

____

<u>**ACTION | Move Forward**</u>

- What are the steps I can take on a daily basis to propel me forward?

____

____

<u>**CONNECT | Who Can Help Me?**</u>

- How can you find the discipline to conquer my goal(s)?

____

____

- What types of coaches might I consider?

____

____

- Who might be an ideal accountability partner?

- What tool will I use to calendar and schedule my day, week, and month?

Chapter 10

Pivot + Adjust

"Like an athlete, as in business and life, one must learn to pivot and adjust." — Debbi DiMaggio

For years, we sat on the sidelines watching our son, Chase, play lacrosse and football. I can still picture him out on the field, helmet slightly tilted, eyes sharp, body in motion, dodging opponents, weaving his way toward the goal. As I watched him, I often found myself drifting into thought. His movements weren't just about the game; they felt like a mirror for life itself. Just as an athlete must constantly pivot, adjust, and find new angles, so must we when life throws challenges our way. Life, like the playing field, is unpredictable.

There are seasons of triumph and seasons of loss, marriages that begin and sometimes end, careers that soar or suddenly shift, friendships that blossom and sometimes fade, and the heartbreak of losing someone we love. Whether the moment is small or life-altering, each requires us to choose: do we push forward, change direction, or simply pause to catch our breath? On the lacrosse field, you see it in every play. The zigging, the zagging, the quick pivots, searching for just the right opening to make the pass or take the shot. Then, there's the team. Each player has a role; each movement matters. It reminds me of the theater, where every actor contributes to the story unfolding on stage. In the end, whether on the field or in life, the lesson is the same: it's not about never stumbling, it's about learning to pivot, to adjust, and to keep moving forward when we do. Even when conditions are not ideal, take advantage of the opportunities in front of you and seize the moment. Personally or professionally, success belongs to those who pivot, adapt, and move forward.

I was skiing down a steep mountain, conditions weren't perfect, the weather wasn't great, and the snow was less than ideal, but I had to make do. Whether on the ski mountain or in life, we learn to pivot on a dime and point ourselves in a different direction. Whether it's on the slopes, in the middle of a big presentation, or in the midst of one of life's major curveballs, it is important to embrace a mindset that keeps you agile and in the game.

Athletes must analyze opponents and adjust their strategies in real time. This ability to think strategically and adapt to changing circumstances is invaluable for entrepreneurs who need to pivot and innovate in response to market demands. In the game of life, being prepared and ready to pivot and adjust is key. Research, planning, and knowledge prepare us and give us the confidence to make the right decisions and the necessary changes when needed.

<u>Keep Your Eye On The Goal</u>

While you pivot and adjust, you must keep the goal in mind, always adjusting toward it. And sometimes, adjusting toward your goal means going around an obstacle or away from the destination to avoid a pitfall before you head back. Take hiking, for example. The most direct path is often not possible or the safest, so you have to switch back and forth, even if that means a more difficult route or a steeper hill.

Relationships may cause us to pivot and adjust at times. Entering a marriage means adjusting to a partnership, while divorce requires a painful but necessary pivot to rebuild independence. At times, friends drift away or grow in different directions. When that happens, we must accept change, mourn what was, and open space for new connections.

Sometimes in life, we experience a job loss or a career change. Being laid off or leaving a long term job feels like we are being knocked of course, but it can also be the opening to a new and even better opportunity. When this happens, we usually come to realize the path we were on wasn't in alignment with who we are any longer, so we learn to pivot and reach toward something more fulfilling.

We, or those we love, may experience illness or injury. An unexpected diagnosis, accident, or even aging can force us to adjust our routines, priorities, and perspective. I vividly remember being diagnosed with thyroid cancer. I was recently married, a new mother, and working full-time. I know all too well about having to pivot and adjust my routine, priorities, and perspective. I was trapped in the hospital with no way out. It was a trying time. But I made it through, as difficult and sad as it was being away from my new family.

Mental health is another area that affects many of us. Periods of burnout, grief, or anxiety often require us to reset, slow down, and reimagine what balance looks like. For overachievers, I understand all too well that slowing down is easier said than done. Life shifts dramatically for those who become new parents. You pivot from a life of independence to great responsibility, learning patience and resilience as you adjust.

Or during the empty nest chapter in one's life, when children grow and leave home, we adjust again, finding a renewed sense of self, purpose, and direction. It may be a bumpy road at the start for some. I know the empty nest all too well and experienced that bumpy road. However, it was the empty nest that propelled me into writing my first book. And into other projects and quests. It took me many years to find my purpose after our kids flew off.

And let's not forget global events like pandemics, natural disasters, or societal shifts, which alter daily life, requiring resilience and creativity. In such times, we are all forced to pivot and adjust. And then there are the little nuisances in everyday life: a canceled meeting, a sudden expense, a change of plans, or a moment of rejection that redirects us, perhaps towards something better.

Just like on the lacrosse field, sometimes life demands a quick sidestep, a zig to avoid a setback, a zag toward a new opportunity, or a pause to pass the ball.

> *"A pivot isn't the end of the goal — it's the refinement that leads you to the right one."*

What Is The Essence of the Goal?

The essence of the goal is this. It's not fixed, it evolves as we evolve. It's not just about achievement, it's about growth through challenge and adversity. It's not just about the destination, it's about the pivots, adjustments, and the people beside us along the way. Just like Chase zigging and zagging on the lacrosse field, our lives demand that same dance, sometimes we dodge, sometimes we pass, and sometimes we shoot. But the goal is never the only win; it's the person we become in the pursuit.

We launched our real estate company in the recession of 2008. Onlookers would ask if we knew we were in a recession because it seemed crazy that we had taken on such a momentous goal during such a significant downturn. My partners and I saw it through a different lens. Although I did have a difficult time making that decision, as I was reluctant to leave our current company because we were doing so well. If it isn't broken, don't fix it. But Adam and our partner Heidi convinced me we should just do it. We spent mornings in our pajamas, after taking the kids to school, discussing, planning, and strategizing before I was comfortable enough to forge ahead. In the end, timing positioned us to take advantage of a great opportunity, to take over an underperforming office in an ideal location. If we had not been in a recession, the investment would have been significantly more, and the opportunity would not have presented itself.

One of my other favorite sayings is to "turn a negative into a positive." Not unlike many other well-known companies that also took a chance during a recession: Airbnb, Uber, WhatsApp, Square, Venmo, Dropbox, Glassdoor, one word spell as is. Brand name Instagram, Nerd Wallet, Stripe, Group on, Pinterest, and Slack.

At the time we were starting HIGHLAND PARTNERS, Adam, Heidi nor I had been utilizing social media, but we quickly learned we had to embrace it because we were launching a company. Our goal was to go from 0 to 100 as fast as we could, just to be known and equal to where we left off. We were top producing agents who had been in the business for many years, but we were launching a new brand that was unknown. As fast as we pivoted, we had to adjust and re-adjust, often. Every day, we made adjustments and decisions, and implemented new programs and new ideas. And we did it. We rose quickly and were on the level of our former companies, playing shoulder to shoulder. As in any sports game, sometimes you win, sometimes you lose, but we were in the game, it was a level playing field, we just had to keep moving forward, and we did. It was actually my son Chase who pointed out this big achievement. My partners and I were entrenched, for so long, with our heads down just doing what we needed to do, never thinking much about the success or taking the time to look back. But we did it; we launched a company during a recession, it was no easy feat, but we prevailed.

"Teamwork makes the dream work. And sometimes, not knowing is our greatest advantage."

I am not sure we would do it all over again if we had known what building a real estate company entailed. Not to mention being taken advantage of by our other partners multiple times over the years. On second thought, perhaps we would do it all over again, only if we did not have to endure the unethical partnerships that were forced upon us.

During the process of building our company, we spent a lot of time in motion, learning everything we could. Embracing social media was crucial, as print advertising was expensive and fading away. Our goal was to rise up and catch the wave. We were agile, scrappy, and constantly seeking opportunities when things fell apart. And sometimes things did. And that was alright; we fixed it and got back on track and figured out ways to do what we needed to do. With a little more research, digging deeper, asking questions, and trying new things, we eventually figured out what we needed.

But don't let the pivot throw you off. Even if you do not feel ready, and you do not yet know how you will adjust, you will. The day we left our old company, we did not leave our success behind; it followed alongside us right out the door. Although I was very uncertain. Our partner Heidi kept reminding me that we were the brand, not the former or even the new company. That was difficult for me to grasp. Now I understand that, but as a young wife and mother raising a family while launching an unknown company, I was tentative. Not only were we introducing a new company to the community while continuing to sell real estate in order to make a living, but we also had to figure out the platforms and tools we needed in our new real estate company including the infrastructure, systems, protocols, and procedures as the leaders and new owners. It went like this: one of our agents would come to us with a need for something, and we'd reply, "We'll get right back to you," and then we'd figure it out. We somehow always found a way.

Pivoting Alone

As my kids got busier in their own lives, all I could see was an empty nest in my future. I wasn't prepared for what was to come and the emotions I would feel. It was during this time that I began searching. I needed a project to move me forward. I just kept thinking, we were once a family of four, soon to be a family of three. It was really, all too overwhelming. What I experienced was very different from what I had understood about the Empty

Nest. My sadness and the feelings I had around the Empty Nest did not begin when my last child left but occurred when Bianca, my first child, left, realizing that soon our son Chase and all of his friends would be gone, too.

One evening at a senior high school going-away party, a father said, 'It's not like she is going off to war.' As crazy as it sounded, his comment put things into perspective and actually made me stop and think. But not for long. For years, I endured sadness.

I spent time going back through family photo albums, assembling a collection of meaningful photographs and creating a memory book for Bianca to give to her before she left for college, although it was really more for me. As I pulled together photographs of family, friends, and Bianca's travels, I wrote captions, sharing words that would hopefully help her with her transition to college and what she meant to me. The captions were as much for me as they were (hopefully) for her.

I titled it, *'What to Share with Your Senior Before They Leave for College.'* I wrote things like… "I love you; we are just a phone call away; try new things, get involved." I cried as I put the book together. When you are one less in a household, time opens up. One early morning, after Bianca had left for college, I began to re-read and write in my journal.

I had been adding to my journal over the years when inspired. I tend to write in the morning before my family gets up and when the house is quiet and my mind is clear. And I love to write when I travel. Over the years, I have assembled a 'Believe' handbook, filled with inspirational words of wisdom. It is something I hoped to share with my children and their friends, and to inspire others who might read it.

The Art of Letting Go: Embracing Life's Next Chapter

Life is a series of chapters, each unfolding with its own beauty, challenges, and transitions. Some chapters we eagerly anticipate, falling in love, building a company, cultivating a career, watching our children grow, while others arrive unexpectedly, leaving us to navigate emotions we never quite prepared for.

One of the most profound transitions in my life was the moment my children left for college. The home that once buzzed with energy, laughter, and the rhythmic chaos of daily life suddenly grew still. Their empty bedrooms stood as silent reminders of bedtime stories, whispered dreams, and a lifetime of shared moments. I had always known this day would come, but nothing truly prepares a mother's heart for the quiet that follows.

At first, I mourned the loss. Not in a dramatic way, but in those quiet moments when I passed by their rooms or set the dinner table for fewer people. I grieved the shift from being the center of their universe to watching from the sidelines as they spread their wings. I found myself grappling with questions: *Who am I beyond being their mother? What comes next for me?* It was in this space of uncertainty that I leaned into the very philosophy I had always embraced, Dream, Believe, Internalize, Share, and Activate. I reminded myself that life is not about clinging to the past, it is about evolving, just as my children were doing. Instead of resisting the change, I chose to reframe it as an opportunity. It took some doing. It did not happen overnight. But I moved through it one step at a time, one day at a time, one month at a time, one year at a time.

I rediscovered passions that had long been set aside in the whirlwind of raising a family. I traveled without schedules dictated by school breaks. I immersed myself in new projects, deepened friendships, and embraced the beauty of reinvention. Most importantly, I gave myself permission to grieve and to grow, honoring both the loss and the possibility. Transitions, no matter how bittersweet, are invitations to rediscover who we are. They remind us that while one chapter may end, the story continues. And if we allow ourselves to turn the page with an open heart, we may just find that the next chapter holds a beauty we never expected.

The Goal

The first step towards my goal (although without much clarity) was to be productive and take my mind off living in a home without children. I wasn't sure what the endgame would be. I kept searching. Sometimes you don't know specifically what the goal is. You know in general terms: "I do not want to feel sad. I want to feel productive and of service." "I need to find a hobby." But you have to start somewhere. You need to begin walking. Once you're in motion, clarity will arrive. Sometimes, you're walking in one direction, and life might take you in another direction. Even if you have to pivot and head in a completely new direction, that's okay.

A podcast I was listening to about meditation pointed out, "If you want a Ferrari, you must take steps in that direction. You can't just sit and wish for it, you have to get up, visit the dealership, test drive the car, and allow yourself to imagine what it would feel like to own it, and next figure out how you can work towards buying that Ferrari." That's how dreams take shape, through action, belief, and movement.

<u>Same Transition, Different Journey</u>

When children leave home, the experience can be profoundly different for each parent and each family. One mother might feel overjoyed, excited for the child's next chapter, and even relieved to embark on her own new journey. Another mother, while happy for her child, may feel an overwhelming sense of loss, like a part of her is missing. The transition can be deeply emotional, even heartbreaking. We all navigate life's transitions in our own time. The key is staying open to support, whether through advice, counseling, friendship, and/or new communities.

At first, I felt like I was in a deep, dark hole. But with time, the support of my husband and friends, daily efforts to try new things, and journaling, I slowly found my way forward. Immersing myself in writing my first book became a transformative experience. Surrounded by encouraging people, I turned my grief into something meaningful. The book not only helped me heal but also became a beautiful way to express my love for my children. It showed them how I transformed sadness into strength, how even the hardest moments can lead to something positive. Writing became my therapy, my healing, and ultimately, a new beginning.

Healing and growth unfold in their own time, at their own pace, as they did for me. Time does heal, and the journey from A to Z is a momentous period of growth. You just need to forge ahead, no matter what obstacles are put in front of you, real or imagined.

Every Milestone Requires A Pivot

The competitive nature of sports instills a sense of resilience. Athletes learn to overcome setbacks and failures, which is crucial for entrepreneurs who often face challenges and obstacles in their journey. Every milestone requires a pivot. Sometimes we choose to pivot and are ready for it; we are ready and willing to make the adjustment, and sometimes it's not a choice; sometimes it's a forced pivot. I have heard, on many occasions, unfortunately, when a husband has said, "I'm done with the marriage," and simply walked out. What do you do?

How is one supposed to get up and pivot from a shock like that? In this generation of text messaging, people are even sending a quick text message when they have made a unilateral decision to break up, oftentimes even ghosting or barely responding. The person just stops communicating, leaving the other party hanging. It is an awful way to experience a breakup, a loss.

Since experiencing the empty nest and having spent years finding my joy again, I find happiness in helping other women thrive after a loss, whatever that loss may be. My fourth book, *Beauty At Any Age, Because Age Is Just An Attitude*, was a prelude to my first book, *Contained Beauty*. *Contained Beauty* was born from loss, a deeply personal expression shaped by grief, reflection, and resilience. As I healed, the story evolved. *Beauty At Any Age* became the next chapter in my journey, rooted in renewal, self-acceptance, and the understanding that beauty is not defined by time, but by attitude, mindset, and how we choose to live each chapter of our lives.

Thus, Beauty at Any Age evolved into a platform to help others redesign, even refine, themselves using my five pillars: Health and Wellness, Beauty, Confidence, Community, and Purpose. When someone is experiencing a transition, it is the opportune time for them to pivot. I have witnessed many friends and clients whose marriages ended, of course, were devastated at the time, but where they pivoted and adjusted to as of today is incredible. Each of them has gone on to do amazing things. The accomplishments are nothing short of magnificent. I hate to say it, but they are all so much better off; I truly believe that.

I told a friend the other day that perhaps it was time to get off the dating app and just live her life. It was bringing her down. I suggested doing what she loved and that she might meet someone while simply being her authentic self in real time, rather than hiding behind an app or a text. I believe, whether in dating, working in real estate, building a brand, launching a company, writing a book, or any other areas in life, if you are doing what you love, you are not only opening yourself up to opportunities but welcoming them with open arms.

I share that same advice when I coach: Do what you love. If you're doing whatever it is authentically, you'll meet like-minded people who are naturally attracted to you personally and in business. No one wants to date or work with an unauthentic, disingenuous person. But you have to get out there and build relationships.

Life Interrupted

"The only way to make sense out of change is to plunge into it, move with it, and join the dance." — *Alan Watts*

Life is sometimes interrupted, not by choice, while at other times, it is intentionally rerouted. No matter where you are in life, whether you're an aging senior, a new mother, newly divorced, grieving the loss of a partner, or adjusting to an empty nest, change is inevitable, and finding a sense of community is essential. I faced this firsthand when our kids left home and quickly realized the importance of building new connections. Likewise, I have an aging friend who has outlived many of her good friends and family members, and with that has been a loss of community. It's not always easy, but here's my message: if you know someone who is alone, regardless of their age, reach out. A simple conversation, a moment of engagement, or a small act of kindness can make all the difference.

Every month, that dear friend, who is well over 80 and I share lunch and run errands together. She often joins me at my open houses, helping distribute real estate brochures. I always wish I had more time for her. Over the past ten years, we've explored various retirement communities, as I believe it's never too early to plan for the future. It also gave us something other to do than just dine out. We kept busy while I was learning about the various facilities so I could better guide my other clients as well.

As the years have passed, my friend lost more and more friends, including her travel leader, who tragically took his own life. He played a crucial role in her life, encouraging her to travel and be in the company of others; his absence was truly felt by her. The isolation during COVID-19 only compounded her solitude. Now in her 90s, she has come to terms with the fact that traveling is no longer feasible. While I've offered to help plan her trips, the real challenge lies in finding the right travel companion, not just someone who can afford to travel, but someone who shares her same travel style. Her husband was her everything, and they traveled often.

I've suggested that she rescue a dog or a cat for companionship, but she humorously retorted, "Debbi, I can barely take care of myself; I don't want a pet!" I found it endearing, but my concern was genuine, I truly wanted her to have a companion. Navigating these transitions was a process, and eventually she put down a deposit on a retirement community. I knew from experience that this would be beneficial for her even though she was reluctant to make the transition. But the time came to adjust on her terms before someone made that decision for her. Today she is healthy, but who knows what tomorrow will bring? (During the writing of this book Velma severely declined and never truly settled into her senior community.) Velma is not social. When I hosted a neighborhood party, she exclaimed, "Debbi, why do you have all these people over?" I explained that it's important for her and the neighbors to get acquainted, especially those who have also lost loved ones. It's essential for you all to connect.

The Decision To Pivot and Course Correct

I, too, had to navigate change when our kids left home. I realized the importance of finding a new community. And that is what I hope for Velma in her new retirement community. It's not always easy, but the message I want to share is this: if you know someone alone, regardless of age or what they are experiencing, reach out; they often just want someone to talk to, engage with, and connect with. Small acts of kindness and companionship can make all the difference.

When we decided to launch HIGHLAND PARTNERS during a recession, that was surely a pivot and a major adjustment. Whether you are going out on your own, starting your own business, launching a company, or were just laid off, or went through a divorce, one question rises to the top: how will I pivot and adjust? What are some tools that might help? Which friends, family members, or colleagues might be of service or have advice? What knowledge and common sense might I leverage? It will not be easy. Many have pulled out of unpleasant situations, but the real growth comes from seeking opportunity and exploring every possibility when you're forced to pivot.

I always say, when the going gets tough, the tough get going. And then I just go. If it happened, it happened, and now it's time to move on. What is the point of belaboring the fact?

"And suddenly you know… It's time to start something new and trust the magic of beginnings."
— Meister Eckhart

"Rock bottom became the solid foundation on which I rebuilt my life." — J.K. Rowling

Another favorite mantra of mine is the three Cs of life: Choice, Chance, and Change. You must make the choice to take the chance if you want anything in life to change. When in transition, whether in business, in the boardroom, on the field of play, or going through a loss, change is the catalyst that propels us into the next chapter, by will or force.

Life's interruptions can come in many forms, each presenting its own unique set of challenges as well as growth opportunities:

- Cancer
- Getting married
- Having children
- Any debilitating diagnosis
- Divorce
- Suicide
- Loss of a significant other
- Loss of a child
- The empty nest
- Loss of a parent
- Job loss
- Job promotion
- Career change
- Relocation
- A new idea

- A new goal

- An aha moment

Each experience, whether welcomed or not, serves as a pivotal point in our story, an invitation to evolve, to shift direction, and to trust in what's next. Change has always been what I love most about life, not because it's easy, but because it's where possibility lives.

Opportunity is the magic of life, it reveals itself in the moments we're willing to pivot, to let go, and to begin again. Without change, there can be no growth; without movement, there is no momentum. Life becomes stagnant when we resist its natural rhythm. So, choose to ride the wave rather than float idly in the sea. Embrace the motion, the mystery, and the transformation that comes with each new chapter. Every pivot is a reminder that you are alive, capable, and always becoming.

<u>Building Community, Establishing Connections. Live Your Best Life, At Every Chapter</u>

"Every new beginning comes from some other beginning's end." — Seneca

"When we are no longer able to change a situation, we are challenged to change ourselves." — Viktor E. Frankl

From the Colombo Club to the Commonwealth Club to Hiking and Eating Clubs, there is a group for everyone.

Research by Harvard Medical School reveals that senior adults with a solid community life are more likely to have "higher levels of physical activity, greater positive moods, fewer negative feelings, and a longer life span."

Now it is your turn.

It's your time and your next chapter to pivot and adjust.

____

____

GOALS | Write It Out

Identify a time when change was forced upon you, and you had to pivot and adjust. How did you work through it? Were you able to pivot and adjust? Looking back, what would you have done differently?

____

____

ACTION | Move Forward

Is there a change forced on you now that you need to prepare for? How can you pivot and adjust? What are some things you can do to help you move through this transition? First off, what do you enjoy?

____

____

CONNECT | Who Can Help Me?

You'll want to connect with others who share your interests. Start by joining groups or activities that naturally bring people together, whether it's cheering for the same sports team, signing up for a book club, or taking a language, cooking, art, or photography class. You might enjoy fitness classes, joining a gym, or getting outdoors with a hiking or gardening club. Explore music or gaming groups, community forums, volunteer organizations, or professional networking circles. You could also connect through cultural or religious groups, pet owner meetups, crafting circles, writing workshops, dance or wine clubs, or even online communities centered on your favorite hobbies or topics. The possibilities are endless, all it takes is a little research and a willingness to try something new.

Take Notes In Your Journal

Key points to consider when choosing a group:

- Interests: Find groups that align with your passions and hobbies. Try Facebook Community Groups and Eventbrite, and start accepting invitations! That is exactly what I did, and that is how I ended up calling LA my second home.

- Location: Look for local groups to meet people in your area.

- Activity level: Choose groups that match your preferred level of physical activity.

- Online vs. in-person: Decide if you want to connect online through forums or meet up in person at events.

- Create a group & choose group settings - Google Groups Help

- How to Make New Friends - WebMD

- Ask ChatGPT: 21 Best Ways to Meet New Friends in a New City or Town

Ready, set, write.

____

____

Chapter 11

Look for Opportunities

"The extraordinary is often disguised as the ordinary — and sometimes as discomfort. When you train yourself to see opportunity, every moment builds momentum." — Debbi DiMaggio

I was living in Goleta with four of my girlfriends from Piedmont, in the small village where UCSB is located right on the Pacific Ocean. I was attending Santa Barbara City College while another group of friends were at UCSB. It is interesting to look back upon my younger years, as mentorship is such a big part of my success in real estate and my personal coaching. I've always had a mentor growing up, throughout high school, and into college, learning from those who trail blazed before me. I chose to attend SBCC following a few of my mentors who had gone before, who attended a city college in order to get accepted into their university of choice. For many of us in Piedmont, that was Cal Berkeley. What I learned was that applying from a four-year university like USD would limit my chances of being accepted to Cal, and going the community college route would be more direct, giving me a much better chance. That is how many of my childhood friends and I ended up getting into Cal.

One of the other experiences I had on my college checklist included an internship in Washington, D.C. From junior high through high school and into college, I had a robust list of things I wanted to accomplish. I am happy to say, I did them all. Prior to my junior year in college, I had my mind set on working as an intern in DC. Back in my first year, after getting an A in Political Science, I contemplated going to law school, which is why I was so interested in working at the United States Supreme Court.

Three of my girlfriends from the University of Santa Barbara (USCB) and I applied for housing at Georgetown University and were accepted. We all wrote letters to firms and politicians, lobbyists, news stations, and the like to solidify an internship before arrival. Each of the three girls lined up jobs prior to our departure. I sent out letters, including one letter to the United States Supreme Court. They confirmed receipt of my letter, but there was no acknowledgement of a job opening. But that didn't dissuade me.

Off we went to D.C., hot, humid, muggy, and rainy. It felt like wading through a warm, murky stew. Summer in DC is fairly unpleasant as far as the weather is concerned, but the city was electric. I wasn't going to let the weather interfere with my goals, especially not one that had become part of my life's mission. Since high school, working at the United States Supreme Court had been written on my list. It wasn't just a dream; it was a decision.

I have always been of the mindset that try, and if at first you don't succeed, try and try again. I know I am fairly strong-minded, even stubborn, and have never embraced the word "no." I dressed up, with the letter from the USSC folded neatly in my leather folder, tucked under my arm, and marched up the imposing marble front stairs to the United States Supreme Court. I am fairly certain that I announced with confidence to the person at the front desk, "I am Debbi DiMaggio, and I have a letter here from Alexander Stevas, the Clerk of the Court. May I see him, please?"

I think it may have sounded more like a demand than a question. They let me in to see the Clerk right away, and I was hired on the spot. It was a wonderful and enlightening experience. Mr. Stevas even asked me to return the following year, but the heat and the summer storms outweighed my desire to return. I am curious; if I had, where might life have taken me?

Alexander L. Stevas served as Clerk of the Court from 1985 to 2016. As I look back, I realize I should have gone back to visit him, as this story comes up every time I reflect back on my life. Clearly, it made a big impression on me and how I think about life, goal setting, and leading with confidence.

The moral of the story is this: I seized the moment. I walked up those intimidating steps into a storied building filled with history and Honorable Justices, and I found the courage to claim my opportunity. What did I have to lose? Many people in that situation would have talked themselves out of it. The key to life is that when an opportunity presents itself, you must take advantage of it and seize the moment, or the moment will pass forever. We all have opportunities; some are more clearly seen than others, and that is why you have to pay attention, keeping your eyes and ears open at all times.

We are surrounded by opportunities almost every day. Whether you're in your office, at a cocktail party, at a networking event, at a meeting, a restaurant, or on the golf course or playfield. Keeping your eyes and ears open is how you will discover opportunities, sometimes strategically; other times, it may be by sheer luck.

Just when you think you know everything about a person or a company or a team, something happens, or you hear something that changes your perspective and opens your mind. The magic is in listening and being open-minded. The worst thing you can do is walk around with a closed mind and a know-it-all attitude. First of all, no one will want to open their mouths around a know-it-all.

Stay Curious

Each week, I attend my BNI, Business Networking International meeting from 7:50 to 9:30 AM. I love how punctual the meetings are and knowing our time won't be wasted on small talk or delays. Every week, each member gives a 45-second presentation. You'd be surprised how much we learn about one another, even though we have been giving these elevator pitches for years. If you listen, you usually learn something new. Oftentimes, as the presenter, you wonder, "What else can I possibly share? But if you share the various aspects of your service, product, or brand, or even about your personal life, something unique might present itself and align or resonate with a particular member that day. For the presenter, this is where the magic happens, turning connection into opportunity and opportunity into referrals that grow your business.

The second component of BNI is scheduling one-to-one meetings. These meetings allow you to go deeper and truly understand the person across from you. Stay curious. Ask thoughtful questions. Listen carefully, and always be on the lookout for opportunity. If you're searching for gold, you have to dig deeper. You never know what someone might say that reveals a need you can help with, or sparks an idea where your expertise becomes the solution. Often, a referral is sitting right there in the conversation; they just haven't connected the dots yet. This happens more often than you think.

Conversations Can Ignite Sparks of Genius

This networking technique can be used in all types of business meetings with colleagues, bosses, and peers, as well as in casual conversation with friends, your spouse, and acquaintances. An opportunity may not be a bumblebee landing on the top of your nose. You may need to look a little harder.

- Be on the lookout for magic and open to the possibilities.

- Opportunities are all around us if we are willing to notice. Always be on the lookout.

- Life is about being proactive. Initiate, be proactive, and seize the opportunities that come your way.

Whether coaching an agent to find success or guiding someone through a transition, my advice is the same. Life is about opening yourself up, whether to gain experiences or to find what inspires and makes you happy. An agent, for example, or any entrepreneur with a service, product, or brand should be networking, meeting one-on-one, and having deeper conversations. Building a brand, your business, or a company requires building your network, your relationships, your team, and your resources. Likewise, if you are going through a difficult transition, it's ideal to get out and get involved, not sitting home depressed. It is no different than a salesperson working from home, not engaging but waiting for their phone to ring. "What are you waiting for?" Instead, you must take action and get into motion.

From Couch to Confidence

After a promising football career was cut short by injury, Lewis Howes found himself broke, aimless, and living on his sister's couch. He had no job, no income, and no clear plan, just a burning desire to make something of his life. But instead of giving up, Lewis started taking small, intentional actions every day. He spent hours studying online marketing, attending networking events, and reaching out to people who inspired him. He used LinkedIn as his first platform to connect and eventually built a business teaching others how to use it effectively.

That consistent effort paid off. Lewis became a successful online entrepreneur, best-selling author, and host of "The School of Greatness" podcast, where he interviews world-class leaders and achievers. What started on a couch turned into a career built on connection, courage, and commitment?

Lewis's story is proof that action trumps circumstance. He didn't wait for confidence or clarity, he built both by taking the next right step. His mantra: "Greatness is not about being the best; it's about being *your* best." Once you see an opening, you must seize it. Once there is a crack in the foundation, you must go for it. Just as an athlete on the field takes the opportunity when an opening presents itself. That is the exact time you must go for it. The alternative is that opportunity will pass you by.

I'll never forget the opportunity that presented itself that one evening at that holiday cocktail party I really did not want to attend. After I met the publisher, Rob Bond by happenstance, not only did I publish *Contained Beauty, Photographs, Reflections, and Swimming Pools*, but with his encouragement, I went on to publish my second book, *The Art of Real Estate*. We also sold his home during this time. Many other opportunities stemmed from that one opening. From that chance meeting with Rob at an intimate holiday party came publishing two books, which led to my third book. A publishing company in Vermont had seen *The Art of Real Estate,* which prompted them to reach out to publish what would become my third book, *Real Estate Rules: 52 Ways to Achieve Success in Real Estate.*

You do not have to be the only one looking for opportunities. Other people or professionals can search for those opportunities on your behalf. Virtual assistants, coaches, talent scouts, headhunters, publicists and other professionals can do the heavy lifting. Years ago, when I worked with a publicist for the first time, opportunities she discovered were already there but she seized them for me. Had she not identified the opportunities, and arranged appointments for me, they would have been missed opportunities that slipped through the cracks. If you are busy focusing on what you do, you often do not have time to do what needs to be done to grow. Hiring a publicist, a coach, social media consultant or virtual assistant can inspire new growth in ways you may not have thought possible or had the time to explore. Hiring the right people to help you grow is key.

I contemplated hiring a publicist for some time, but I wasn't certain it would be fruitful. I decided to give it three months. I hired Liz Kelly, who soon after became a dear friend of mine. I rarely meet anyone who does not become a friend. Working with Liz was like waking up on Christmas morning every day. Liz would come to me with unique ideas and opportunities. My husband and I held interviews, we were written up in magazines, and she solidified two online publication writing gigs for me, among many more. I loved walking through those unknown, new doors every day. It was exhilarating.

One of the more interesting opportunities I experienced was attending Celebrity Gifting Suites during Emmy and Oscar Week. The gifting suites are a way to celebrate the nominees, actors, actresses, and others in the TV and film industry through the build-up weeks in advance, promoting the nominees and their films. As a vendor, like myself, it provided us a way to engage a target audience who is there to learn about your product, service, or brand while taking candid photos with you. At first, I was reluctant to participate, so I provided 100 copies of my book, and one of the models handed them out. I was pleasantly surprised to see how the celebrities posed for pictures with my book. I caught Dot Marie Jones sifting through my book during lunch, and she asked if I had published it. She had nothing but compliments and kind words. I continued to see Dot Marie for years after that, during the other gifting suites I participated in.

Life as a Series of Stepping Stones

Life unfolds like a series of stepping stones, one right in front of the other. Once you open your heart and become aware of the possibilities around you, the magic begins. One thing leads to the next. Once you take that first step, that small, intentional act, your next opportunity suddenly appears.

When you walk through one door, keep going. Another door will open, and then another. That's the beauty of momentum, it builds upon itself. I'm reminded of a video game Chase and Adam used to play when they were young, called *Star Fox*. Looking through the *Mindset in Motion* lens, I can see now that it wasn't just a game; it was a lesson. Star Fox had to keep moving forward, always looking for the opening, flying through one portal to reach the next level. That's life: each door leads to another challenge, another discovery, and another chance to level up.

It's the same in *Mission Impossible*, type movies, the hero is constantly moving, adapting, and overcoming a new challenge. Every mission presents a new hurdle, but the hero always finds a way out or through. Life mirrors that rhythm. It's a journey of stepping stones, filled with hurdles, opportunities, and unexpected detours. Some doors will close; others will open wide. The key is to stay alert and notice that sliver of light, that possibility just waiting to be explored. And when there isn't a door in sight, create one.

Contained Beauty Book Passage

At every chapter in our lives, we go through changes, some welcome, others maybe not so much. Life's transitions are inevitable, yet how we navigate them defines our resilience and growth. Over the years, I have undergone my own transformations while navigating the various chapters of my life. As a mother, friend, and coach,

I've encountered many individuals along the way. I've witnessed their struggles, offered support, and successfully guided them as they faced and overcame challenging moments. As much as I tried to speed up their healing and offer next steps, I came to realize it's a process they must go through on their own. Healing and self-discovery require personal effort, whether through soul searching, therapy, a new hobby, or engaging with a supportive community. Friends and family will try to help, but sometimes those we love are just not ready. It's up to the person to reach a point where they are open to receiving support and guidance.

I recall a conversation with a friend about her 'aha' moment. Over the years, I had shared insights based on my own experiences, but she wasn't ready to receive my thoughts and ideas at the time. After going through her own transitions and doing the work for herself, she finally understood the guidance I had offered years earlier. It was only when she was ready that she could fully process and embrace her healing, her changes, her growth, her next chapter. It takes time before one is receptive to receive.

We all move at our own pace, but we do not have to navigate transitions alone. But we all need a sounding board, whether it's through friends, therapy, the right professional assistance, or self-reflection.

<u>Healing Through Contained Beauty</u>

I spent a year producing a book, which in hindsight was a year of therapy wrapped in a project. It was the way I worked to heal myself from the sadness brought on by the empty nest and how I navigated this transition. Everyone has their own way to heal; some go to therapy, while others find their own ways to transition and move forward.

Key Aspects of Transition:

- Grief: Understanding the stages and finding ways to cope.

- Reality vs. Not Reality: Distinguishing facts from emotions.

- Moving On: The importance of closure and forward momentum.

- Community: Finding strength in collective support. Community is a crucial key factor throughout our lives and into our golden years, as well. We all need 'community' to thrive and to survive.

- Projects: Engaging in creative and meaningful endeavors.

- Journaling: Processing emotions and tracking growth.

- Hobbies: Rediscovering passions that bring joy and purpose.

- Friends & Family: Recognizing and leaning on your support system.

- Support Groups: Connecting with those who understand your journey.

Reflecting on Your Own Transitions

Take out your notebook and map the journey that shaped you using the prompts below. Let's take a moment to reflect on the significant chapters you've experienced:

- Leaving, or graduating from high school after 12 years, stepping into the unknown.

- College: Leaving behind a core group of friends and professors, and navigating your independence as a young adult.

- Designing your 20s: Discovering identity and purpose.

- Breaking off an engagement or longtime relationship, facing heartbreak and redirection.

- Marriage: Embracing partnership and growth.

- Parenthood: The miracle and challenges of raising children.

- Health Battles: Facing cancer or other illnesses.

- Loss: Coping with the impact of suicide and grief.

- The Empty Nest - Redefining identity after children leave home.

Action Steps:

- Share - Open discussions can provide insight and validation.

- Discuss - Explore perspectives, both personal and professional.

- Reflect - Journal your thoughts, fears, and aspirations.

- Brainstorm - Identify actions and individuals who can help you through transitions.

Journal Entry:

- Write down a few transitions I have experienced.

____

____

____

- Brainstorm steps to navigate my current or upcoming transitions.

____

____

____

- Identify people, resources, and communities that can support me.

____

____

____

Life's transitions are not meant to be faced alone. By embracing each new chapter with an open heart and a willingness to grow, we find the strength to move forward with grace and resilience.

Practical Actions To Seek Out Opportunities

Get in motion. When a friend, Realtor or coaching client comes to me with a problem, roadblock, or a goal, I focus on getting them into motion by starting with a list of what they want to do and identifying what is holding them back.

Motion Creates Action to Motivate

Motion is the beginning of transformation. It's the shift from thought to action, from intention to energy in motion. When we move, we awaken something within ourselves. It's not the other way around. We don't wait for motivation to strike before taking action, it's through motion that motivation is born. A simple step, no matter how small, creates momentum. That movement builds confidence. Confidence fuels courage. And courage propels us toward our goals, even when the path isn't yet clear.

Just as I did when I set out with a goal to write my first book. Or when I began contemplating the idea of hosting a podcast. Every action, whether it's making the call you've been putting off, writing the first line of a new chapter, or simply getting out the door for a walk, activates energy. It tells your mind and body, *I am ready. I am moving forward.* The morning I walked out the door to run in my neighborhood while pondering what Chase meant when he said he wanted to challenge himself. I had no idea I would go on to run a marathon less than three months later. It certainly was not on my mind that day, but as I pushed myself forward and got into motion, thoughts and ideas transpired into a desire to do more.

When you move, you shift your state, mentally, emotionally, and physically. You break inertia. You turn resistance into rhythm. You invite clarity, flow, and purpose. So don't wait for motivation to appear. Create it through motion. Let movement be your spark, the force that transforms thought into progress, and progress into power.

Renew Your Personal Space

Rearranging your space can help bolster inspiration. I am constantly rearranging the furniture in my home. Currently, my dining room is in my living room. During COVID/Shelter In Place, I must have reworked our spaces five times. On a basketball court, coaches are constantly repositioning the players to maximize effect, just as moves are made on a chessboard in order to unlock opportunities. Whether we are tossing ideas around, readjusting our position, rearranging furniture, or asking questions, each of these actions leads to movement. The same is true with learning. You can open a book, tune into a MasterClass or a podcast, engage in meaningful conversation, or even discover insight tucked inside the lyrics of a song. Inspiration is everywhere. The goal is to see things in a new way, from a new perspective, from a different angle in some way you have not seen before.

When Edison was working on the light bulb, he had trouble finding an element that would conduct electricity without immediately burning out. As he unsuccessfully tested thousands of elements, it would have been easy for him to give up. But thankfully, he kept going. He had a vision, and he believed that his vision could become reality. So he tried element after element until he found one that could sustain the electric current. It is said that in the end, he tested 10,000 elements. When asked about his 10,000 failed experiments, he said, "I have not failed. I've just found 10,000 ways that won't work." This reinforces the importance of dedication, persistence, and a strong desire to keep going without giving up, even in the face of resistance.

Renewal Through New Perspectives

Travel has a wonderful way of helping us renew our space. It's like stepping onto a plane and landing in a new country, everything feels different. The air, the sounds, and the rhythm of daily life shifts our perspective and awakens our senses. Details are noticed that once faded into the background, and suddenly, the world feels alive again.

For me, living between two cities, Los Angeles and Oakland with my husband Adam, offers that same sense of renewal. Each environment has its own energy, pace, and inspiration. The change itself becomes a teacher. When I transition from one place to another, I see things through a new lens, and that simple shift opens my mind to new possibilities.

But renewal doesn't always require a suitcase and a plane ticket. Sometimes, the opportunity to refresh our perspective is right where we are. It begins with curiosity, the willingness to look at the familiar in an unfamiliar way. You can travel without moving an inch. Watch a travel video on YouTube, learn about a culture you've never experienced, take a language course, or rearrange your living space to create a new flow.

Renewal is less about the destination and more about perspective.

When we intentionally seek new ways to see, we create movement, internally and externally. That movement is what keeps our *mindset in motion*.

Identify What You Need

Use your journal as your compass. Begin each morning by writing, before the day rushes in. Let your thoughts, dreams, and questions flow freely onto the page. As the day unfolds, return to your journal whenever inspiration strikes, jot down a fleeting idea, a moment of gratitude, or a new realization.

Whether you're writing in a beautiful notebook, typing in your iPhone notes, or capturing thoughts on your laptop, what matters most is *getting it out of your head and into motion*. Writing clarifies what you truly seek. It transforms confusion into clarity and ideas into action.

"*Writing is movement. The moment you put pen to paper, or fingers to keys, you activate focus, energy, and forward momentum.*"

<u>Be Open to the Conversation</u>

Where would you be if someone did not give you an opportunity? That's why it's so important to be on the lookout for opportunities. Ask, reach out, and connect. The following are three life-changing pieces of advice.

1. No one knows what you need until you ask. Our parents, teachers, husbands and wives, bosses, partners, therapists, or friends, even strangers cannot possibly know what you need until you enlighten them. I have asked people I do not know for assistance and most responded in the affirmative!

2. You do not need to know everything; you just need to know where to go to find the answer. This same sentiment crosses over into all aspects of life and in business. It's not unique to real estate. I find myself offering this piece of advice to new agents quite often: if you do not know the answer, simply let your client know that you will circle back shortly with an answer or a solution.

3. Even if you are not sure, take a few steps and see what happens. Every year, I strive to achieve a goal or try something new. It can be big or small. Running the LA marathon and multiple other races dominated 2024. Writing books satisfied me for a few previous years. Attending celebrity gifting suites for a few years, and then one year I contemplated launching a podcast. I was not convinced I was actually going to do it because I am not fond of speaking to the camera. But I had written books, so it only seemed a podcast was the likely next big thing. Not long into thought mode, I propelled myself into motion, by taking action through research, meetings, and conversations over coffee and lunch dates, phone calls, and Zoom, all the while keeping an eye out for an opportunity. Beyond staring into a video lens I was very concerned about the technical part of hosting a podcast. As I was in motion, doing the work, being curious and asking questions, I began receiving emails and noticing information on podcasting had entered my orbit. I had many conversations and learned quite a bit, but wasn't entirely convinced. Until this one producer reached out after his AI program discovered an Oprah interview I recorded on YouTube over 15 years ago. Upon speaking with him, I felt very comfortable with the process. When he explained that the production company would implement the technical production and posting, and my only technical part was to log in, I was sold.

The important part of this story is that I was not yet sold on launching a podcast. I was in *research* mode, I was *in motion, and I was open to the opportunities*. But not until I spoke with John did I see it truly happening. The moral of this story is get your feet wet, wade in the shallow end, test the waters, but keep an eye out for that awesome wave coming your way, and ride it out.

4. My superpower is my *insatiable curiosity*. I've always been drawn to people, to learn where they come from, what drives them, and to understand the story behind who they are. Curiosity is what connects us, and that is what energizes me each and every day.

Through my podcast, I have the honor of meeting incredible individuals from around the world. Each week, I have the privilege to listen, learn, and share their stories, and that, to me, is a true gift. Hosting *Mastering the Art of Real Estate and Mastering the Art of Success* has opened countless doors, not just to conversations but to opportunities, inspiration, and lasting friendships.

One of my favorite encounters was with Mike Paul, "The Fix-It Guy," The Reputation Doctor for celebrities, CEOs, and other public figures. I met him by chance one Sunday afternoon while sitting with a friend watching a football game at the Claremont Hotel. He happened to be next to us, so we struck up a conversation. At first, I wasn't planning to invite him to be on my podcast, but when he began engaging on social media, I thought he would be the perfect fit. He shared podcasts he'd been featured on, so I took it as a sign, an opportunity, to invite him on mine, and soon after, he became one of my guests. Had I not been paying attention to our brief meeting that Sunday afternoon and a few long-distance pings here and there, I would not have invited him on my podcast, *Mastering the Art of Success*. Nor would he have become someone I now can call a friend. And if you need a 'Fix It' guy, give Mike Paul a call.

"Relationships are created through chance meetings and seized opportunities. Every day I wake up excited to see what opportunities may come my way."

My video coach, Kim Rittberg once asked who I'd like to interview. Instantly, I thought of a talented interior designer from Australia whose work I'd admired on YouTube. That episode was such a joy. Her story began during COVID when she was encouraged to start a Vlog by her daughter, proof that courage and creativity often bloom in uncertain times.

While writing this book, I found myself prompted by my own words to reach out to Bob Burg. I asked if he might introduce me to anyone who would be a good fit for my podcast, *Mastering the Art of Success*. To my surprise, he said he did. As you may know, Bob Burg is a renowned author, coach, and speaker, and I might have been reluctant to email him had I not been guided by the very principles I'm sharing with you here. How could I fall short of the actions I encourage others to take? So, I did it. And the result? Success, a response. A reminder that nothing ventured, nothing gained.

That's the beauty of *curiosity in motion*: when you follow your instinct, stay open, be brave, and have the courage to ask. People may say, yes, they may say no, but there is never harm in asking; only growth, connection, and the magic that comes from taking that one small, bold step *forward*.

Build Momentum

When you say *yes* to opportunities, it builds momentum. When you say no, the door is closed. It's over. **Momentum is your secret weapon!** Start small, stay consistent, and watch your progress snowball. Whether it's a morning workout, tackling your inbox, or taking steps toward a bigger goal, each action builds momentum.

> ***"Progress builds confidence. Confidence drives success."***

When you're in the mindset of seeking and seizing opportunities, you begin to recognize opportunities and possibilities, everywhere, not only for yourself, but for others as well. Be generous in sharing those opportunities. Open doors, make introductions, and lift others as you rise. We all move further, together.

Experiencing Loss and Seizing Opportunities On Our Own Time

Loss isn't always about death. Sometimes, it's the quiet shift that happens when life changes shape, when the children we raised begin to live their own lives, when a relationship fades into routine, or when a once-busy schedule suddenly becomes still. These moments can feel like standing in the middle of a familiar room that no longer feels like home.

A few years ago, a friend of mine was going through the loss of no longer having her daughters with her. She wasn't grieving anyone, yet grief lived in her bones. The children had grown and moved on; her days were no longer dictated by carpools or school calendars. The silence that followed was unfamiliar, both freeing and lonely. She filled her time with new projects, classes, and plans. For a while, it helped. But no matter how much she tried to fill the space, the ache of "what now?" remained.

There were days she felt inspired, alive with possibility. Other days, she questioned everything. Who was she now, without the roles that once defined her? Was this what reinvention looked like, or was she simply lost? Over time, she began to notice something shift, not all at once, but gradually. In the stillness, she began to listen. She journaled, she traveled, she reconnected with friends. She explored meditation, movement, and moments of joy that didn't depend on anyone else. Slowly, she began to understand that loss wasn't the end, it was an invitation. An invitation to rediscover herself. To rewrite her story. To begin again. When we experience loss, of a person, a purpose, or a chapter of our lives, we are not meant to fill the space immediately. Sometimes the void is where we find our voice. And one day, we wake up and realize we've crossed into something new. Not the life we had before, but the life we were always meant to live next.

I recall a pivotal point when things turned around for her. During one of our many conversations, she said, "You were right, I just wasn't ready." I had shared my experiences and what I thought she should and could do, but we ebb and flow in our own tide pool on our own timetable. She had to go through her own journey. The important thing was that she was in motion and trying new things, which helped her gain clarity, come out of depression, and reinvent herself.

My journey is uniquely mine, just as yours is uniquely yours, and we each turn the page and enter a new chapter in our lives on our own time. I had experienced my own version of loss, for me that reinvention came through journaling, experiencing new things, joining various clubs, manifesting and affirmations, a gratitude practice, multiple courses, writing, and more writing, a mindset shift, pushing myself, saying *yes* when I wanted to say *no*, traveling, following my daughter half way around the world, to Australia, and then to New York, until eventually finding a reprieve and new community in LA. Don't get me wrong, I would still do it all again; I'd move through it with the same openness — but without the heaviness that once accompanied it. It's not about holding on to every moment of my children's lives, but about creating my own.

"Progress begins with adjustment. Opportunity belongs to those who move before they feel ready."

Forward Motion Is the Antidote

<u>GOALS | Write It Out</u>

Reflect on where you are right now.

- What door have you recently walked through?

____

____

- Which next step is calling your name, even if it feels uncertain or small?

____

____

<u>ACTION | Move Forward</u>

Take one simple step forward today, send the email, make the call, research the idea, or reach out to someone who inspires you. Trust that each action activates the next opportunity.

____

____

<u>CONNECT | Who Can Help Me?</u>

Share your next step or an "open door moment" with a trusted friend, mentor, or one of your communities. Momentum grows when we move together, one step, one door, one level at a time.

<u>Further Thoughts and Action Items</u>

Don't stop. Let your ideas flow.

Chapter 12

Half-Time Pep Talk

Courage to Act:

"Failure isn't final. It's an invitation to rise, recalibrate, and move forward." — *Debbi DiMaggio*

"Success is not final, failure is not fatal: it is the courage to continue that counts." —Winston Churchill

"Our greatest glory is not in never falling, but in rising every time we fall." —Confucius

Story adapted from "The Inspirational Story of the Greatest NFL Comeback Victory" by Yue Wu, originally published on Medium.

On a cold winter day 30 years ago, two American NFL teams were battling it out in New York's Rich Stadium for playoff glory. NY's Buffalo Bills were the underdog hosting the visiting Houston Oilers, who had previously bested the Bills in a 27–3 victory in the last regular season game the week before. On top of that, the Bills lost their starting quarterback, Jim Kelly, to injury, so the backup quarterback, Frank Reich, started this critical playoff game. The first half seemed to have confirmed the Bills' worst fears as the Oilers raced to a 28–3 lead. Heads were low, and bodies were limp as Bills players filed into the locker room for the halftime break.

And then, something happened to the Bills team. Even as the Oilers extended their lead to 35–3 after the start of the 2nd half, the Bills stayed resilient, and the whole team came out fighting together, with the defense shutting down the opponent and the offense finding creative ways to score. In a span of just under 7 minutes, the Bills scored 28 points or 4 touchdowns. The team went on to tie the game in regular time, went to overtime, shut down the Oilers' opening drive, and won the game with a field goal. This marked the first and only time an NFL team came back to win after a 30+ points deficit in a playoff game. History was made!

So what happened in that locker room during the halftime break? What can we learn from it that can help us to turn things around in our 2nd half? In the Bills locker room during halftime of the playoff game, Bills Head Coach Marv Levy challenged the team: "You've got thirty more minutes. Maybe it's the last thirty minutes of your season. When your season's over, you're going to have to live with yourselves and look yourselves in the eyes. You'd better have reason to feel good about yourselves, regardless of how this game turns out." He then took quarterback Frank Reich aside and reminded Reich of what he had done in college football. It turned out Reich was the quarterback of the Maryland Terrapins, who were down 0–31 against the Miami Hurricanes at halftime and fought back to win the game 42–40. That was the biggest comeback in college football history. Bills coach Levy said to the quarterback Reich, "Maybe lightning will strike twice." And strike twice it did! **With an inspired team who are playing for their pride and a quarterback who was reminded of his biggest moments from the greatest comeback in college football, the Bills made NFL playoff history as the only team to ever come back from a 30+ point deficit.**

"Focus on the next play."

In an extended interview about the Greatest Comeback game, Frank Reich shared a few interesting insights about how he achieved the historical feat. "Just focus on the next play." Frank's suggestion also happens to be the most effective and actionable step you can take when facing an almost impossible challenge. When you are in that predicament, negative emotions like anger, fear, anxiety, embarrassment, and disappointment are probably running wild in your brain. They cause formidable interferences to your cognitive functions and make it nearly impossible for you to concentrate. By focusing on the next play, you are redirecting your brain's attention to things within your control — the plays that the team had practiced hundreds of times. In fact, Frank remarked that when they did the no-huddle offense, everyone had to be super focused, and the team got into a "flow" state where they just clicked: each person knew where they needed to be and what they had to do. And each play they successfully completed increased their confidence.

One of the most impressive displays of team productivity was during a span of 6 minutes and 53 seconds, where, at halftime, the Bills scored 28 straight points, and this was after they suffered an embarrassing score to the Oilers, who intercepted a Frank pass and returned for a touchdown to make it 35–3. When Frank asked about this impressive feat, he actually thought it was the Oilers that made it possible.

On the sports field, as in life, it does not matter what the score is at halftime; one must not accept the current circumstances. Once you do, its game over. As in my story, had the players accepted the score at halftime, they would not have pushed through and prevailed. This chapter is about playing through to the end and not a second sooner.

We can experience a comeback in the boardroom, on the sports field, even within a marriage if we come at it with dedication, persistence, determination, and desire.

"Success is the sum of small efforts, repeated day in and day out." —Robert Collier

Facing Rejection and Finding Momentum

One of my coaching clients faced rejection after rejection when she first entered real estate. She struggled to find clients and worked a part-time job to make ends meet. Frustrated and disheartened, she felt stuck. After a year or two of going through the motions, with no success, she decided to give coaching a try.

Once we began our coaching sessions, you could see she was starting to gain momentum. Through weekly meetings, accountability systems, and a mindset shift, she persisted, and eventually prevailed. Today, she is a full-time real estate advisor; she quit her part-time job and is enjoying her dream job, helping clients and friends with their real estate goals. One of the best feelings as a coach and mentor is witnessing the success of another person. It takes hard work, time, effort, and the right mindset, but once she chose to commit to a routine and a plan, to create that momentum, things started to happen.

Oftentimes, people throw in the towel before they even begin. They might try something for a while, but when they don't see quick results, they say, "Maybe this is not for me." Fortunately for my friend, she decided not to go back to her paying day job but to forge ahead and get the help and guidance she needed to launch. I encourage others not to settle or resolve to accept their situation; instead, move yourself forward, and do not concede too early in the game. Don't quit before you even begin. Whatever that is for you in life, personally, professionally, in work or play, push yourself a little harder, a little farther. On the flip side, if you are far ahead in the game or in life, I warn against getting too comfortable, arrogant, or overconfident and letting your guard down.

I vividly recall a game when Chase's football team faced a tough opponent. As it turned out, Chase's team built such a commanding lead that the coach put in the second string. By the end of the game, they had lost their advantage, and the game. I was frustrated; I can only imagine how the athletes felt. The team was playing well, they worked hard to outmaneuver their opponents until the coach undermined their entire game by letting his guard down too soon.

The moral of this story is that you must play your very best until the bitter end. How many games have been won or lost in the last seconds? It's exciting to witness, but not so fun if you're in the game, or it's your life.

When you are coming up from behind. It is difficult when you are down, and you do not see any light at the end of the tunnel, but this is the exact time you must not let your guard down. Don't throw in the towel too soon, raise your head high and play, plan, plot and strategize until the very end.

When the going gets tough, the tough get going, and push even harder.

I embrace this mindset, especially when the real estate market takes a turn, or we move into that holiday slowdown. Rather than take a seat and rest on my laurels, I use this time to regroup, focus on marketing and thanking our clients –past and present for their loyalty and friendship.

Q: How can you use a slowdown in your personal or professional life to stay in momentum?

____

____

As I wrote this chapter I heard the most profound episode on Bob Burg's, *The Go Giver* podcast. As I say when this sort of serendipitous moment happens, *coincidence, I think not.* An article once written about me in UNIQUE HOMES magazine was perfectly entitled, 'Accidentally with Purpose' . The editor really hit the nail on the head when she gave it this name. The same goes with this story.

A very distraught father was saying goodbye to his 14-year-old son, who had been in the hospital for over 100 days. As the doctors informed him that his son had only a short time left to live, the father called his brother to say he wouldn't have time to come and say his goodbyes.

Shattered and not knowing what else to do, the brother sat down on his couch and recorded a video, sharing his grief and desperation. I imagine he said something like, "My nephew is dying. He has this rare disease. Is there anyone out there listening and do you have any advice?" What happened next was beyond anything he could have imagined.

While the father sat by his son's bedside, completely focused on being present, his phone began to vibrate, again and again. Reluctantly, he finally looked down to find message after message from doctors around the world, reaching out to help. The father quickly connected these doctors with his son's medical team, and by some miracle, the boy was saved. If this isn't an example of *playing through to the end*, I do not know what is.

Half Time, A Time To Re-energize and Re-Group

Why is halftime so important? In sports, halftime offers a crucial opportunity to pause, reflect, and reset. Similarly, throughout our lives, we experience our own "halftimes", moments when we must step back, evaluate where we are, and decide how to move forward. These pauses are essential for us to regroup, refocus, and realign with our goals and purpose.

When we hit an age milestone, it is not uncommon to look back five, even ten years and evaluate what we've accomplished, or perhaps what we have avoided. During a marriage or long-term relationship, we may quietly reassess who we have become within that partnership. When a marriage ends in divorce, the reassessment deepens, we are not only grieving the relationship, but we are redefining our identity, routines, financial foundation, and future vision.

When an entrepreneur pours heart, time, and resources into building a business that ultimately fails, that moment can become a defining crossroads, a humbling pause that demands recalibration, renewed belief, and the courage to begin again, wiser than before.

The following are three companies that repositioned themselves for success:

Starbucks: The coffee shop which now inhabits every street corner (and sometimes two on each street corner) did not always sell fresh-brewed coffee to customers. They started off in 1971 selling espresso makers and coffee beans, which Howard Schultz (current chairman, president and CEO) fell in love with on first taste. After his visit to Italy in 1983, Schultz was determined to actually brew and sell Starbucks coffee in a European-style coffeehouse, and transformed Starbucks into the nationwide java sensation it has become today.

Nintendo: We all know Nintendo for innovating and inspiring an era of mass-produced video games, such as Super Mario and Donkey Kong. However, the company existed several centuries before that, and dabbled in producing everything from playing cards to vacuum cleaners, instant rice, a taxi company and even a short-stay hotel chain (also called a "love hotel," I'll leave it up to you to figure out what that is). It was in 1966 that Nintendo started producing electronic games and consoles, which gained wide popularity over the following 30 years.

Instagram: Instagram is the most widely used photo app for iPhone, but many don't know its origins. Instagram began as Burbn, a check-in app that included gaming elements from Mafia Wars, and a photo element as well. The creators worried Burbn had too much clutter and potential actions, and would never gain traction. So they took a risk and stripped all the features but one: photos. They rebuilt a version of the app that focused solely on photography—it was clean and simple, and clearly it paid off.

Here is a list of ways one might navigate life's pivots during "halftime":

- Reset
- Re-align
- Re-evaluate
- Re-energize
- Regroup
- Shake it off and identify what didn't work out
- Identify what works and what's not working
- Drop it and move on; drop the negative attitude, don't accept it
- Make a change if a change needs to be made
- Losing steam? Pump yourself up by getting into motion
- Rest or pause, if you're burning out.
- Take breaks.
- Use strategies to make those breaks effective.

- Ask for help if you need it from coaches, professionals, therapists, friends, or colleagues.

- Rebound

- Reward yourself – celebration creates energy.

- Energy creates results.

Halftime is a good time to reevaluate. It is the time to identify what is halting your momentum and do what needs to be done to keep moving forward. Address the issue, forget what happened yesterday or last week, press reset, and move on.

Entrepreneur: Someone who jumps off a cliff and builds a plane on the way down. An entrepreneur doesn't let a simple roadblock deter them from their mission or goal.

You will fall off the wagon, you will miss a workout, and you will deviate from the plan; life happens. This is why "halftime" is so important; it is the time to regroup and move forward. Don't beat yourself up; just get into motion even if your direction is still unclear. Have you ever been on one path, moving one way, towards one goal, and then something happened that inspired you to move in a different direction? This book was inspired in just that way.

On a Sunday afternoon my husband and real estate partner offered to host our open house. I agreed; after all, I had hosted our open house the day before. As I sat in my favorite room in our house looking out at the crystal clear blue sky and the San Francisco Bay with sparkling city and three bridge view, I could not help but be inspired. I was scrolling through Instagram and came across a profile for the third or fourth time. The man appeared to be a surfer, and he was sharing his success, yet I was unsure what he was selling, so I dug a little deeper. He was promoting a TEDx preparation course. I decided that was most likely the next big thing for me to conquer. Aside from my ongoing real estate career of 35 years, having written five books, launching my own podcast, and running the LA Marathon, I found myself back in discovery mode. So I bought the course. And in true Debbi, aka Droid Mode, I opened up the course and started doing the work. I was immersed in the course all afternoon. I believe it was the next morning, after having taken pages of notes, when I realized I needed to find more clarity. I had so many ideas, but what I really needed was one topic to explore, fine-tune, and develop into a 15-minute passionate talk that would flow like a waterfall. Looking down at my notes, it was at that point I realized I had to write another book. I needed to find clarity. I knew if I was going to do this thing, I had to be crystal clear on a single topic and choose just one aspect of the topic I would share. And within 24 hours a new book would be put into motion. At that time I did not know it would be this book.

The key takeaway: Even though you are not yet committed and are unclear of your direction, it is only in motion when clarity begins to unfold and manifest.

Halftime is the *check-in, it* is that pause along the way. It is the time to reassess and contemplate. Do we want to edit our plan of action or move forward? I liken it to skiing. When skiing down a mountain, we eventually get to a fork in the trail. This is when my husband and I stop, look around, and then decide which way to go. We may even discuss it. Depending on particular circumstances at the time, we may opt for the Double Black Diamond, opt for the Blue Trail, or aim for the Green route, the easiest way down. If we are just starting out the day, we may choose the more difficult route, but if it is at the end of the day, circumstances will be different. Are we tired? How do our legs feel? Is the snow slushy or icy?

I have always embraced a mindset that giving up is simply not an option and that pushing through is the only way. And, searching for your own path is the way. You must pivot and adjust your mindset in order to play your absolute best, until the end.

Oftentimes, people self-sabotage during a losing streak, whether they're down points in a game, struggling in the classroom, facing setbacks at work, or healing from a breakup or loss. When doubt, fear, or a sense of unworthiness creeps in, it can quietly pull you off course. But just like in sports, halftime is not the end, it's the reset. In life, as on the field, your comeback begins the moment you choose to believe again.

The importance of working on yourself to build the necessary skills will allow you to receive the outcome that you want and deserve. According to various research, a significant portion of people tend to give up on a goal when they are close to achieving it, with estimates suggesting that around 90% of people fail to reach their goals, often quitting when they are nearing completion, sometimes referred to as the "almost there" phenomenon; this is particularly prevalent with New Year's resolutions, where many people abandon their goals within the first few weeks.

Lesson: Success Through Persistence

Success doesn't require getting everything right the first time, it demands resilience and consistency. Like Thomas Edison, who failed a thousand times before inventing the light bulb, true success is built on lessons learned from setbacks.

Success is rarely the result of one bold move; it is built through steady persistence. Persistence is not stubbornness, it is disciplined commitment. It is choosing to stay in the game when progress feels slow, when doubt creeps in, and when results are not yet visible. But persistence alone is not enough. If you are carrying inner blocks against success, fear of visibility, fear of failure, fear of outgrowing your current identity, no amount of effort will produce the results you desire. Halftime is where you recognize what is holding you back. It is the moment to reflect, recalibrate, and reconcile the beliefs that are limiting your growth.

You must be in the game to identify those blocks. When you are actively participating, you can see your hesitation, feel your resistance, and assess your performance in real time. From the sidelines, there is no feedback and no transformation. In the arena, however, every experience becomes data. You learn what strengthens you and what weakens you. You adjust. You recommit. Persistence then becomes powerful because it is aligned. Success ultimately belongs to those who stay in the game long enough to confront themselves, grow through what they discover, and keep moving forward.

Halftime is the point in the game where gaps are identified, addressed and realigned.

Now that you've identified your limitations, roadblocks, and mindset patterns, you have something tangible to work on and the opportunity to reconcile your goals while gaining clarity, direction, and results. It begins with asking for help and guidance. As mentioned in previous chapters, coaches and specialists exist in many forms.

Here is a quick list:

- Therapists, Psychologists, Hypnotherapists, and Shamans

- Healers

- Acupuncturists, Chiropractors

- Coaches: There is a coach for nearly every need, from professional and business growth to personal transformation. Whether it's life, leadership, fitness and nutrition, mindset, accountability, financial strategy, speaking, relationships, or performance.

- Reading and listening to books
- Joining groups and communities
- Engaging in conversation
- Listening to podcasts
- Attending seminars
- Attending networking events

"Success happens not despite failure but because of it." —Winston Churchill

What Does Winston Mean?

Failure as a stepping stone: Instead of viewing failure as an endpoint, see it as an inevitable and necessary part of the journey toward success.

Learning opportunity: Each failure provides valuable lessons and insights that can be used to improve and adjust your approach to achieve your goals.

Resilience and persistence: The core message is to maintain your enthusiasm and drive even after setbacks. It emphasizes that it is the courage to keep going after a failure that truly defines success.

Growth mindset: The quote supports a "growth mindset," where one believes that abilities and success can be developed through dedication and hard work, which includes learning from one's mistakes.

<u>One Cannot Force Learning Nor Action Upon Another</u>

As we move through the pages of our life, you, your friends, family, and colleagues will be in different places, both mentally and emotionally. We all arrive at our destination on our own time. Over the years I have watched friends and colleagues experience changes, where they were at one time and where they ended up, but the change and evolution occurred on their own time. No matter how much we seek to help, guide or lead, another person simply cannot effect change on another. "You can lead a horse to water, but you cannot make it drink."

It is incumbent on a person to make their own decisions, to be their own advocate, and to be their own catalyst for change. Believe in yourself, and align your thinking of success and your ability to do it, whatever that is for you. Least of all, you do not need to go it alone. Take the time to find and align yourself with professionals and experts, mentors and coaches to guide, coach, and inspire. But in the end you must be the one to put in the work.

"You are not waiting on fate. Your future responds to your choices."

Many examples and stories can be cited of people who overcame trauma, some with the help of professionals, and others on their own volition. Take, for example, Dr. Joe Dispenza when he heard the words from his doctors that he would never walk again. After a serious spinal injury, Joe Dispenza used meditation to heal himself by mentally rehearsing walking again, focusing on a clear, uninterrupted image of his healthy, and healed spine. He dedicated two hours a day to this visualization, and within 10.5 weeks, he was back on his feet, eventually returning to work. He believes this process involved intentionally shifting his thoughts and emotions to align with his desired healing, which in turn influenced his body's biology.

The story of Dr. Joe illustrates not giving up when you're down. Being open to a new outcome, not self-sabotaging, and being willing and open to receive a new result. He also focused on himself, working on behalf of his own interest while dismissing what did not suit his vision.

I completely subscribe to this thought process. The mind is a powerful tool, we just need to use it. **The coach is not always right.** Oftentimes we may see things from a new or different perspective than our partner, superior, boss, manager, coach, colleague, or peer. Process what they are telling you, but if you believe something to the contrary or even wholeheartedly disagree, it is your responsibility to speak up for yourself, your teammates, and your colleagues.

Second Opinions: Always advocate for yourself and seek the best information available. Don't accept a diagnosis or conclusion without question, explore your options. Take action, seek therapy, physical therapy, and get the support you need. Talk to multiple professionals, explore new methods, and stay open to what might work for you. Talking things through with others can lead to new insights and unexpected results. Remember, don't throw in the towel before you've tried everything. Persistence and curiosity can make all the difference in your healing and growth.

Halftime Reevaluation to Reset and Regroup

No matter how hopeless you think your situation is, there is always a way out or a way through. If you truly desire a change, there is a way out; you must find that way. You must cultivate a level of belief beyond where you are, or think you are; work hard, keep a positive outlook, and lean on your support system.

Many groups and communities exist for that one specific "thing" you are experiencing. When my friend lost her taste buds to COVID, there was even a community for that. Another friend was taken for hundreds of thousands of dollars by a fraudulent Coinbase company, and she found a community that led her to an international attorney who is an expert in overseas fraud and embezzlement cases. Whatever you are going through or need today, there is a community. There are numerous platforms offering support, shared stories, and community, as well as feedback, guidance, resources, and recommendations.

In closing, halftime is the perfect moment to pause, pivot, and reassess. If you find yourself unhappy, whether in a relationship, your home life, or your current chapter, seek alternatives. You deserve joy, not misery. Gather the support and resources you need to make a change and step into something better. If the empty nest has arrived, divorce is at your doorstep, or a relocation is in your future, let each day become an opportunity for activation, moving you from sorrow to motion and, ultimately, into joy.

And remember: change doesn't happen overnight. Transformation requires repetition, consistency, and patience. Small, deliberate actions taken every day create the momentum that drives change.

"Clarity sets the direction. Discipline sustains the journey. Persistence delivers the outcome."

<u>GOALS | Write It Out</u>

- What do I need to reassess in my personal life today? Am I happy, or do I want things to change?

____

____

- What do I need to re-evaluate in my professional life today? Am I happy, or do I want things to change?

____

____

- What do I need to do to move forward >>>>> What am I currently doing or working on where I know I need to change direction or update a goal to move forward?

____

____

<u>ACTION | Move Forward</u>

- Write out everything I desire to do and to have in my personal life.

____

____

List out everything I desire to encompass in my professional life. What types of people do I want to be around?

____

____

- What environments do I thrive best in?

____

____

- Write, edit and rewrite my goals; daily, weekly, monthly and that one big goal for the year. Include a 5 and 10 year plan. Do what you can but write out at least one goal.

____

____

CONNECT | Who Can Help Me?

- Personal Goals: Identify someone, or more than one person, in my immediate family, inner circle, or someone I look up to who can help me move the needle forward.

____

____

- Professional Goal: Identify someone within my office, networking group, or extended professional circle, or ask a colleague or friend for an introduction, to connect with an individual I don't yet know but would like to meet.

- Schedule a meeting with any or all of these people to review my goals and discuss key questions related to my professional growth.

____

____

- Goal Setting and Business Planning: Download a goal-setting planner or business plan workbook. Many can be found on Canva; within your own office, and with a simple Google or AI search, you will have many at your fingertips.

____

____

I'd love to hear your thoughts and what you learned, as well as any small wins and big successes you achieved from this and other exercises in this book. Share, comment, or ask a question on Instagram @DebbiDiMaggio or www.DebbiDiMaggio.com

Chapter 13

Play to the End

"Shoot for the moon. Even if you miss, you'll land among the stars." — *Norman Vincent Peale*

The Last 10% Takes 90% of the Effort

I've known many friends and family members who have summited grand, intimidating peaks. It's not easy. Oftentimes, when you find yourself at the end of a game significantly behind, or at the end of that figurative rope, you may want to throw in the towel. Even when you're within close proximity to the top of the mountain and considering giving up, don't.

But, when you are near the end, deep in the fourth quarter, or down at the half, now is not the time to quit! Chin up, breathe in, exhale, and focus. No doubt you put a significant amount of thought and effort in from the beginning, you owe it to yourself to push on and do what you have to do. Chat amongst your teammates or your partner, or look inwardly towards yourself.

When I was running the LA Marathon and was past the halfway mark, around mile 18, but nowhere near the finish line, my inner voice and I were having a lively discussion. Unless I became ill, tripped, was injured, or was no longer able to run, I was absolutely staying in the game and would not cut my race short. The conversation was not, *"Should I continue, or should I call it a day?"* That little thought-bubble ticker tape continuously scrolled: *"You are not an almost, a could-have, or a would-have." " You do not quit what you begin."*

I visualized the rest of the run in my mind's eye, and believe me, driving that route takes time. Running it is an entirely different story. But I did it. One step, one mile, one decision at a time. During the editing of this book, I was chatting with my colleague, Jesse, when he asked if I had hit the wall at mile 18. I answered, almost curiously, that yes, I did. Then I asked him what that meant. He shared what his marathon runner friends had explained: mile 18 isn't just fatigue. It's a sharp physiological and psychological breaking point.

I had been telling my story about what happened to me at that exact mile, never realizing it was actually a phenomenon. My friend **Ellie** once shared a story about when she and some friends hiked Mt. Baldy, named for its steep, treeless slopes and among the most dangerous hikes in the country, peaking at a summit of 10,064 feet.

They were worn out, and their legs were like noodles. They were losing steam and strength. However, Ellie and her friends chose to support one another through it. They took smaller strides and stopped more often to catch their breath. I don't know about you, but for me altitude is a trigger for one horrific headache that can last days. In the end, Ellie and her friends did what it took to acclimate, they were patient and took the time to breathe while supporting one another even though they were too tired to speak. Here's where collaboration and camaraderie ensued.

Most people give up right before they're about to achieve their goal. My son was hiking one of the 53-58 named peaks in Colorado that are over 14,000 feet, known as "fourteeners," and one of their buddies just could not summit along with his friends, even though he was extremely close. He had two choices, attempt his goal, and succeed or attempt his goal and become worse off. We all need to know our limits and when to call it to avoid injury, even hospitalization. When snow skiing, I often call it a day hours before the lifts close; the altitude can be harsh. Know your limits, and decide when they're meant to be stretched. Before you fall back, consider your options. Think of the hard and tireless work you've put into the game, your business, marriage, or relationship.

"The true reward isn't simply finishing, it's knowing you showed up fully, with heart, grit, and purpose."

Very few people will actually achieve their goals. You are in the minority if you do. Those who play to the end are the people who excel in life personally and professionally. Most goals don't fail because of a lack of desire. They fail because of a lack of structure, accountability, and disciplined execution. When goals remain vague, untracked, and unsupported, even strong ambition fades.

<u>How Do You Go About Playing until the End?</u>

A few important strategies can help you make it past the finish line.

- The power of keeping your mindset in motion, moving through to the end.

- Don't take anything for granted. Keep moving forward and play until the last second; take every opportunity.

- Lean on your team whoever that is, depending on your specific goals.

- Celebrate small victories.

- Take breaks as needed and jump back in.

"You don't quit when you're tired. You quit when you're done." — David Goggins

"When you feel like quitting, remember why you started." — Anonymous

"Pressure is a privilege—it only comes to those who earn it." — Billie Jean King

These quotes resonate deeply with me. When I was running the LA Marathon, I felt that my ability to run was a privilege. At mile 18, as I repeated to myself, *"You finish what you begin,"* I also reminded myself, *"You are fortunate to be able to run. You are running for those who cannot, or those who are sick or disabled."*

Those thoughts propelled me forward, through mile 18, past mile 19 and beyond. I was filled with gratitude and driven by something bigger than myself. Surprisingly to me it was actually quite an emotional experience.

"Even when you believe victory is assured, the final seconds demand every ounce of focus."

Key Statistics

Games are won and lost during the last second of the game. It is not uncommon for a tie to ensue in the last few minutes of a game, or for one team to be slightly ahead of the other only to lose the game in the last minute with a touchdown or goal. I've seen it on TV and in person. The moral of the story: play your best until the end.

I am very stubborn when I want something. A client was working with another real estate agent, and she eventually was referred to us as everything seemed to be going awry. The company sold her house without providing a clause giving her and her family time to find a replacement home. The client called us to see if we could possibly find her a home in the highly competitive market we were experiencing. Shortly after she came to us we made an offer on a property. At first, we didn't get it. The agent texted me to say we had lost. I could not nor would not accept her answer. I was driving when I received the news, so I pulled over and called the agent right back and told her emphatically that our client and her children really needed the home and to please call the other buyer and let them know that it was they who lost. I do not know to this day how I convinced the agent to call her seller back and then call the buyer to tell them they lost. But she did, and our client won the house. I am still not quite sure how I did it.

"Tenacity matters. It doesn't guarantee a win, but anything worth winning is worth striving for."

- In sports analytics research on "safe leads" and lead changes, one study (by Safe Leads and Lead Changes in Competitive Team Sports) found that the probability a given lead is *truly safe* depends heavily on its size **and** the remaining time in the game. *They show that leads early in the game are much less meaningful than leads late in the game*, and there is a bimodal distribution of when the **last lead change** tends to occur—often very early or very late. arXiv

- The same study analyzed ~1.25 million scoring events in ~40,000 games across multiple sports and found that the risk of losing a lead remains significant right up until the end of the game if the time remaining is short. arXiv

- In basketball, the concept of the "buzzer-beater" (a shot made just as the game clock expires) is well documented, though precise league-wide percentages of games ending on buzzer-beaters are less frequently aggregated.

A *buzzer beater* is a shot taken at the very last moment of a game, released just before time expires, that determines or changes the outcome.

Here's a well-known example: In the 1998 NBA Finals, Michael Jordan's final shot with the Chicago Bulls—made in the closing seconds against the Utah Jazz—sealed the championship. It's often referenced as the ultimate buzzer-beater moment: **calm under pressure, decisive, and game-ending.**

"In life and business, you don't celebrate the lead, you protect it until the final second."

Those who do not see their goals through to the end have their reasons, or is it a list of excuses? The question is, are you someone who quits when the going gets tough, or are you of the mindset to play until the final second? Which of these reasons resonates with you?

- Too tired.
- Don't have the time or energy.
- I can't.
- Doubt if I can even do it.
- Re-evaluation. Is it really that important to me?
- I don't have the support. I really don't want to bother anyone or ask for help.
- I am not that motivated.
- I just don't have enough discipline.
- Talk yourself out of it.
- Imposter syndrome.
- Not enough confidence.

- Lack of preparation.
- Listen to naysayers.

When you read this list, what comes up for you? Is it laziness, or are you disorganized? Is it a lack of true desire? Is winning or conquering that goal just not as important as when first initiated? When I coach, I notice one commonality that repeats. *I just don't have time.* Some exhibit a lack of follow-through, or is it laziness? If you follow the concepts in this book, you will find success, but you have to put in hard work and effort. A car cannot run on an empty tank. If you truly care and have a real desire to succeed, you will *find the time.*

As a self-proclaimed control freak and someone who is obsessed with follow-through, it is very difficult for me to relate. As Will Robinson often says, "That does not compute."

Exercise

Was there a time you gave up in the last 10% ?

List the reasons you did not finish.

____

____

What could you have done differently?

____

To combat this, try and push the negative self-talk aside and continue moving forward. You can stall out, but get back in the game.

<u>The 5 R's: Strategy for the Last 10%</u>

Noted below are five steps to help you play to the end when the mountain in front of you seems daunting, whatever that 'mountain' may be.

This reminds me of my running races, and how I routinely kicked up my heels and ran even harder the closer to the finish line I got.

Reflect

- Look back on your purpose, your goal and your why.

- Reflect before you give up, is it really something you want to give up on? Maybe it is but maybe it is not. Really take the time to contemplate before you give up.

Reiterate

- A business partner, colleague, expert, or coach, family member, mentor or friend. Surround yourself with a strong support group. An accountability partner, team, or group is one of the most effective ways to stay focused and follow through.

- Motivate and boost one another. During a running race, you see your running mates, you actually don't see the people falling behind or quitting. When you are in a pack and doing "it" together that motivates and keeps you on point.

- Teamwork makes dream work, doing something together even if it is side-by-side with a stranger. We are stronger together, much more motivated and less apt to quit.

- Don't let your guard down. Stay on top of your game.

- Keep trying new approaches. Edison didn't stop at the first failed experiment. Apple reinvented itself after near collapse. SpaceX pushed forward after multiple failed launches. Success is rarely about the first idea, it's about the discipline to keep refining until it works.

Resist

- Resist the temptation to quit or give up.

- Resist the temptation to start something new or different.

- Resist the opinions of others, and most importantly, the naysayers.

Reframe

- Pivot and Adjust. If you need to take a step back to realign, even reach out for assistance.

- Take a day off, take a break. Sometimes we just need to stop what we are doing and give ourselves time away to regain clarity. When we do we come back stronger than ever.

Reenergize

- Stop to catch your breath and then move on again.

- Keep moving forward, and do your best not to overthink.

- Remember, finishing the game matters. Playing through to the very end.

The end of the game isn't truly the end, it is the beginning of what comes next.

<u>Every Finish Line is Simply the Starting Point for your Next Chapter</u>

You will not get to the post-game if you don't finish the game. If you quit before the end, it's as if you never did it at all. If I had stopped halfway through the marathon, I would not have run the marathon. I would have spent all that time thinking about the marathon. I may not have trained for it physically but it did preoccupy a lot of my daily thoughts mentally, as I read books, contemplated how I would feel and questioned, would I even be able to finish the race. For weeks before the race, the thoughts alone took up space, and a surprising amount of energy.

Think back to all the work you've done thus far, all the work you've put into something. Whatever "it" is, consider the time and energy wasted if you give up too soon. To get to this point, no doubt took a tremendous amount of thought and energy, maybe even money. In a marriage, you go through years of being engaged in a partnership and/or part of a family. Do you want to give that up without a fight, or at least trying? In a career, you certainly exert exceptional time and energy. You have to ask yourself, do I want to start from ground zero? Or should I attempt to work things out?

Embrace the Possibilities: Go All The Way!

"New beginnings are often disguised as painful endings." — Lao Tzu

"Your present circumstances don't determine where you can go; they merely determine where you start." —Nido Qubein

Life is divided into chapters, each offering unique opportunities for growth. By shifting your mindset, staying accountable, and following a structured process, you can navigate transitions with greater ease and purpose. Playing to the end is the Activate step's final demand, the unglamorous stretch between starting and finishing where most people give up.

<u>GOALS | Write It Out</u>

What will I believe is possible for me today?

____

____

<u>ACTION | Move Forward</u>

What is the one step I can take to move toward it? Because when I believe in myself and act on that belief there is nothing I cannot conquer.

____

____

<u>CONNECT | Who Can Help Me?</u>

____

____

Call To Action: Unlock your true potential. Dream big, believe in yourself, share your journey, take action, and align your life with purpose.

The next chapter is waiting, step into it boldly.

PART 3
Post-Game

Chapter 14

Post-Game Mindset

"Losing doesn't define you. How you respond does. This is where belief begins."

"You don't rise by avoiding failure. You rise by learning to stand taller after it."

The end of a game provides an opportunity for reflection. Whether things went exactly according to plan and you "won," or everything fell apart and you "lost," it's vital that you give yourself the space to reflect, regroup, recenter, and redefine your goals before you move forward.

Games have seasons just as professions have seasons, usually a busier and a slower season. Each game has its own season, including playoffs and the championship game. It is during the off-season that the hard work is put in so that you can prepare for the busy season. It's not a time to fully unplug because preparation is the key to success. The holidays are usually a slower time for those of us in real estate; it's our off-season. Unlike many who slow down, this is where I continue to put in even more time and effort. My schedule may differ as well as my activities, but building relationships and keeping top of mind is important in real estate as it is in all businesses. I find it enjoyable; it is what I am passionate about. It is my life. The slow season is less hectic; it's an ideal time to book coffee and lunch dates, a time to celebrate with friends and clients, and even a time to share gratitude and appreciation.

"Don't delay, level up. Those who excel are the ones doing the work in the off-season, learning and improving while others sit on the sidelines."

Life has a rhythm, it ebbs and flows. I've learned to trust that over the years and not get depressed or feel a sense of hopelessness. In a commission-based business like real estate and similar careers, it can be difficult to remain positive when the season slows. But, just like nature, we move through seasons that shape us, strengthen us, and remind us that transformation is always possible. When we stop fighting the season and start honoring it, life feels lighter, more meaningful, and even more peaceful.

Spring: When Possibility Blossoms

Spring is that spark inside us, the moment something new whispers, *"Try me."* For me, spring shows up as an idea during a morning walk, a conversation that lights me up, or that quiet nudge telling me it's time for a change. Spring is hope. Spring is energy. Spring gives us permission to begin again, no matter where we are in our story.

Summer: The Season of Momentum

Summer is when we're in motion. We're building, expanding, creating… saying yes to the things that feel aligned. It's the hustle, but the good kind, the kind that comes from passion rather than pressure. Summer is full, warm, and abundant. It's where your effort meets your excitement, and you remember why you started in the first place.

Autumn: The Courage to Let Go

Autumn has always been one of my favorite seasons because it teaches us how beautiful releases can be. Leaves fall not because they're failing, but because they're preparing for what's next. In our lives, autumn is that gentle (or not-so-gentle) reminder to let go of old expectations, old habits, and old stories. This is the season where clarity appears. And with clarity comes peace.

Winter: The Quiet of Becoming

Winter can feel slow, still, and even uncomfortable. But winter is where the real work happens, the internal kind. It's where we regroup, rebuild, and get honest with ourselves. It's planning the next chapter, dreaming bigger dreams, and allowing ourselves to rest without guilt. Winter is the season that prepares us for our next bold move.

Honoring Your Current Season

As humans, we often want to live in perpetual summer, always producing, always achieving, always in motion. But that's not where growth happens. Real change comes from honoring every season, especially the ones that feel tough or unclear.

Every season has a purpose. Every season brings you closer to who you're becoming.

Ask yourself:

- What season am I really in right now?

____

____

- What is this season trying to teach me?

____

____

- Where can I soften? Where can I stretch?

____

____

When you understand your season, you understand your path. And that is where transformation begins. In sports and in nature, the "off-season" is where the foundation of growth is set. A cherry tree does not bear fruit if its roots don't get covered by ice during the winter months. A sports team is only as good as its preparation. By the time an A-list actor enters a set, he has studied the script, every scene, and every relationship and has _become_ the character he's playing.

Ellie's niece has been competing in dance since she was 11. During the pandemic she was 12, an average dancer.

Her mother created a dance studio in their living room so she could spend six to ten hours per day dancing and taking lessons. She really leveled up. Two years later, when she started high school, she auditioned for the dance team and made the varsity team as a freshman. A huge feat for a freshman. Even birds will use the slow seasons to practice their dances by watching and mimicking adults, often practicing their routines with peers. This practice is crucial for developing the complex courtship displays used to attract mates, with some species like the bird-of-paradise even perfecting their performances for years before they begin mating. Other birds, like albatrosses, work together as pairs to refine their unique dance sequences.

Take this time to identify what in your life has come to an end. Was it a relationship, a job, a business? Learn from it and strengthen your mindset. You are resilient, you will bounce back. Today is the day you write your next chapter. What did you learn? What could you have done better? Write down your thoughts and reflections in your notebook. This is the core of the post-game mindset. It is in the slowing down and through reflection that we gain more clarity. As in my first book, *contained beauty, photographs, reflections, and swimming pools,*

I note the Taoist proverb,

"No one can see their reflection in running water. It is only in still water that we can see."

Growing Through Wins

At the end of the year, when the holidays are upon us and business slows down, I like to regroup and see what I can do to make the next year even better. The year-end is an ideal time to review your current strategies, see what worked best, and see what may need improvement. It's also a wonderful time to build new and deeper relationships. During this time, when business is slow, you can keep your calendar full with coffee appointments, lunches, and afternoon tea, weaving these social visits between your holiday shopping. Make it fun. Building relationships should be enjoyable, not hard work. It's an ideal time to catch up with past clients, forge new relationships, and create lasting connections.

Growing through a win is about setting oneself up for success. It's about aligning our mindset to succeed. 'Growing through a win' can be understood in two powerful ways. On a literal level, it evokes the image of plants thriving in the sunlight that streams through a window, an invitation to create a window garden bursting with herbs, flowers, or small vegetables, especially for those with limited outdoor space. Metaphorically, it speaks to the idea of recognizing every *win*, every opening, opportunity, or moment of clarity, as a place to grow. Just as plants can also flourish under intentional artificial grow lights, we too can cultivate growth year-round by creating supportive conditions within ourselves. Whether through natural light or by designing the right environment, growth is always possible when we choose to nurture it. What mindset can help you stay agile and teachable when you are already succeeding? Ask yourself a few questions:

- Could I have improved my performance?
- What could I have done to improve?
- What might I have done differently?
- What can I add?
- What might I take away?
- Where did I lack enthusiasm?
- What was my attitude like?
- How did I react to and treat my peers, my coaches, my boss, my partner, my employees, my friends, or my family?

Letting your guard down can be both good and bad, depending on the circumstances. If you've done something well, even had a stellar performance, you will want to repeat it. How can you do it again? First of all, don't be arrogant. Depending on the situation, you may or may not want to let your guard down. If you are on the playfield, you most definitely do not want to press pause. When trying to break down barriers or walls and get close to another person, you may have to become somewhat vulnerable to let them in and to really see you.

As an athlete, I went as far as I could easily without much effort. I was a natural athlete. What I came to learn and see over time was that my teammates were improving faster than I was. I actually stagnated while they excelled.

I am speaking of my young age and experience as a gymnast. I think about those days in elementary and junior high school often. Although I was only between the ages of 10 and 14, I recall the lesson as if it were just yesterday. Later in life, as my own children were involved in sports and other activities, I continually shared my story with them, as they too had natural abilities, and I never wanted them to look back and think, "I could have done better."

Do not take your job, relationships, or talent and wins for granted. You must keep working and forge ahead; continue to excel, or eventually, you will fall behind, become lazy, or even take things and people for granted.

Growing Through Losses

Imagine a locker room after the team just lost, not just the game, but their confidence, their rhythm, their spark. The room is quiet, filled with that heavy air that only follows disappointment. The coach does not storm in. He does not shout or blame. He stands there for a long moment, letting everyone feel the weight of it. Then he says, "You know what this feeling is? It's not failure; it's feedback." Every head turns as he continues, "This, right here, is the moment most people quit. They label it defeat, walk away, and tell themselves it wasn't meant to be. But champions? They do something different. They sit with the loss. They ask what it's trying to teach them." He looks around the room. "Every setback is a mirror. It shows us where we hesitated, where we doubted, and where we stopped believing. That's the real opponent, not the other team, but the voice in your head that says you can't come back." His tone shifts, calm turning into conviction. "So we are going to learn. We are going to pivot and adjust. And next time, we are going to walk onto that field not hoping to win, but expecting to because now we know what it takes." He smiles, and something shifts. "Losing doesn't define you. How you respond does. This is where belief begins." That day, the team doesn't just rebuild a strategy, they rebuild a mindset. When the next game comes, they play with calm confidence, grounded in one truth: "You don't rise by avoiding failure. You rise by learning from it, and standing taller the next time."

The Real Pivot Story Behind Twitter

In 2005, Jack Dorsey was working at a company called **Odeo**. Odeo was a podcasting platform. At the time, podcasting was new and exciting. Then Apple announced that iTunes would support podcasts directly. That move crushed Odeo's business model overnight. Imagine building a company around podcast distribution… and then Apple steps in and integrates it into iTunes. Game over. So the founders (Evan Williams, Biz Stone, Jack Dorsey, and others) realized they had to pivot, fast. And that they did.

Don't take a win for granted, or a defeat as a loss. A positive mindset does not end when the game ends. A growth mindset does not cease when you're still striving to attain your goals. You must continue; you must persist, endure, and motivate, whether you've won or lost or hit a bump, or major pothole in the road. It is guaranteed in life that you will have setbacks. You will experience setbacks as a child and well into adulthood, from not being chosen first and even being chosen last, or not at all. That feeling will sit with you for a lifetime. But that feeling is what will propel you forward, a reminder that you do not want to be that person. You want to, and you can be more. It'll happen in teen relationships, and as young adults and in marriage, people change, and relationships ebb and flow just as seasons do. You might not get that raise or promotion, or the funding, you might not get the job, the contract or the opportunity, but as on the sports field and in life, each day is an opportunity to hit the reset button and begin again.

A Setback Is a Setup for a Comeback

Failure is where you dig deep down inside, level up, and rise to the occasion. It is when you must strike out with a razor-sharp, positive mindset and continue to work through until you succeed. Ups and downs are part of the equation; you will fall down, you will stumble, and you may not be chosen or fought for, but it is your responsibility to get back up again. It's on you to drum up the courage and the right attitude, just as a bull in a bullfighting ring with its eye set on the muleta.

Oftentimes, we get to the end of a game, whether it's on the field, in business, or in our personal lives, feeling like we didn't play our best. We may feel defeated, embarrassed, or tempted to throw in the towel. These moments happen to all of us. When they do, I suggest hitting the pause button.

Take a moment to step away. Shake it off. Go for a run, cry, or scream, if you need to. Allow the emotional release without judgment. Then take a deep breath, inhale slowly, exhale, and give your nervous system a chance to reset. Do this a few times, letting your breath slow your adrenaline down. Close your eyes if it helps. If you need to, slip into another room or even a bathroom stall to regroup; do it. Your first job is to calm your body so your mind can catch up.

Once your body begins to settle, you create space for clarity. This is the moment when emotions no longer lead the conversation, you do. From here, you can shift out of reaction mode and back into your power. Before you move into the next step, give yourself a moment of self-compassion. Offer yourself the same grace you would extend to someone you love. Everyone has off-days. Everyone makes mistakes. These moments do not define you, they refine you.

Breaking It Down To Build It Better: Clarity Before the Comeback

Be open to constructive criticism and willing to hear perspectives that may be uncomfortable. Approach the conversation, whether with a coach, a business partner, or a loved one, with curiosity instead of defensiveness. A simple framework can help:

1. Ask: "Can we walk through what happened together?"

2. Listen: Allow space for honest feedback without interrupting.

3. Reflect: Repeat back what you heard before responding. This strengthens clarity and trust.

We might carefully choose our words, soften our delivery, and lead with clarity and calm, but ultimately, we can only speak our truth, offer our best advice, and act with integrity. At some point, we must release what is beyond our control. Not every conversation will land perfectly. Not every person will hear us the way we intend. And not every interaction will result in the outcome we imagined. But each exchange gives us a chance to learn, to refine our communication, and to stay rooted in who we are, regardless of how others respond.

This approach keeps the discussion collaborative rather than combative, creating room for growth instead of guilt. When you pause, breathe, give yourself grace, and then choose to engage with intention, you transform a tough moment into a powerful turning point.

Growth Happens When We Don't Succeed

Remember the times you won big and headed off to celebrate. Of course, we should celebrate our wins, both big and small. But if you win all of the time, you do not get the opportunity, nor have a reason, to stop long enough to review, learn, change, and grow. Story after story tells us that many successful people failed first, while some failed over and over again until something big eventually happened. It is through constant refinement that momentum is created and propels us forward, physically, mentally, and emotionally.

Losses prepare us to rise up again. As I like to say, don't get mad, get even! We do become better, stronger, and more prepared through our failures. It may not be fun, but it is a part of life, and it will repeat time and time again.

Expect failure as part of the equation, factor it in and be ready for it. It's not something to fear; it's something to leverage. Wear your failures as a badge of honor. They are the lessons that set you free and move you forward. How many times have I replayed a business conversation in my mind, trying to figure out why it went so poorly or why it didn't unfold the way I hoped? I've lost count. It's human nature to revisit those exchanges, searching for the moment everything shifted. Did I say the wrong thing? Did they misunderstand my intention? Could I have presented my ideas differently? It can be incredibly frustrating, because no matter how prepared we are or how thoughtful we try to be, we still cannot control how others will react, respond, or receive our message.

The end of a game is not the end, it's the opening to your next chapter.

The end of a game is actually the moment you decide how you will rise. It's the time to reflect back, to identify if there was anything you could have done differently. It's a time to step back, regroup, talk it through, take a pause, and meditate on it.

<u>What Mindset is needed to Look Back Effectively</u>

- Be willing to take constructive criticism without feeling as if you are being attacked.

- Have an open mind

- Be teachable

- Don't blame others

- Take responsibility

- Be able to learn from your mistakes as well as your successes

- Don't make rash decisions or say things you'll regret later

- Be willing to retrace your steps.

- Successful athletes and business people alike break down their weaknesses and successes to determine what needs fine-tuning.

- Identify what you did right, even if it was a complete failure or disaster. As well as if it were a success.

- Take notes, write it out, internalize it, and feel it.

- Trace a better outcome in your mind by reimagining the event

- Don't give up. Get back on the horse or in the ring, and try, try again

- Put yourself into motion, especially if you don't feel up to it

In sports, the time clock designates the end of the game. In life, it may be the end of a job, the collapse of a company, or the closing of a chapter, which shows you the door signaling your time to move on. Ask yourself if you've exhausted every possibility. More often than not, we know in our gut when it's time to move on from a personal or business relationship. You know when, after you've exhausted every aspect and looked at the situation or relationship from many angles. And you will know when you've truly given it your all, and the time is now. Our intuition is usually spot-on.

In life, we may not have a clock or a stopwatch, but our intuition usually knows when something has come to an end.

Don't throw up your hands or concede too soon. Pause until you've examined things from all viewpoints. If you are still unsure if it is time to give up or throw in the towel, maybe it is time to reevaluate. Start from the beginning and go through the *Mindset In Motion Method*™. Check yourself. Go through your morning and evening routines. Take space and time to think about it. Separate yourself from that thing you're considering ending and closing the door on. Life is not made up of starts and stops with a halftime buzzer. Life is not made up of periods or halves or quarters. Life and relationships ebb and flow. And as we ebb and flow, we need to pay attention. We cannot take what we do and who we spend time with in life for granted.

In the end, whether you've lost the game or you are innately aware that a relationship is coming to an end, in a job transition, or didn't get the deal, the promotion or funding, continue to work at, keeping a positive mindset, knowing that you are simply moving into the next, best chapter. To a better place where you will discover more opportunities. Take the time to fight to play another game, live another day, and explore and experience a fresh, new phase in your life. Do your best not to be negative or self-deprecating.

Just as there is a next season, there is always another game, another opportunity, another job, another relationship.

"We broke up."

"The stock market is down."

"The real estate market is awful."

"Interest rates are up."

"I hate my job."

"I lost my job."

"We didn't get funding."

But life happens. That is guaranteed. I have always subscribed to the premise that *when the going gets tough, the tough get going.* Likewise, in a down market, or any other obstacle, real or imagined. *It is the fuel that revs the engine and gets the motor running.* All you have to do is implement and activate; and in that moment you may not believe you just need to do something! Eventually, you will see results, you will believe again and be encouraged to move forward.

"Motivation is the fuel that propels us into motion."

Get up, get dressed, and get out, even when you do not feel like it. The key is not to overanalyze or try to talk yourself into action or out; simply get into motion. As Kris Kringle says to the Winter Warlock in *Santa Claus is Coming To Town*, just "put one foot in front of the other, and soon you'll be walking out that door."

Sometimes The Game Isn't Over

Oftentimes we can repair the damage done and work towards making a situation better or improving it slowly over time. For instance, when you've said something bad or definitive, it's more difficult to get back on track. Most likely, you know yourself and how you act and react in certain situations. I know what pushes my buttons. For me, it is the time to stop and breathe, maybe take a short pause or even sleep on it before heading back to address a particular conversation. When we give ourselves time and space to think, review, and reflect on what is happening, it is amazing what we can learn. Of course, some situations are out of our control, but that does not mean we have to compound the pain by saying or doing something we will later regret.

How To Apply This Strategy

- ### Relationships: Schedule An Appointment

How can we move forward after a disagreement or a betrayal? The key is to know what pushes your buttons and what pushes your partner's buttons. Lay out a plan for the next conversation, just as you would schedule a therapy session. Book a time that works for each of you without distraction, and commit to the date and time behind closed doors.

- ### Business: Reflect and Review

Whether you have been in business for a week, months, years, or for decades, it is always good to reflect and review, even if the action, the meeting, or the sales call was a success. We learn in reflection, not in moving forward.

- ### Presentation: Rewrite

You gave a big presentation; parts of it were right on, and other parts were a miss. Again, take the time afterwards to review and even recite the entire presentation to work out what you might have done differently. Rework the presentation in writing while it is fresh in your mind, making any and all corrections, edits, or improvements before you move on.

<u>Review, Reflect, and Refresh</u>

Looking back I realized it was the in the writing of *Contained Beauty* that was a part of my healing process, although while in motion I was not aware that's what was happening. I wrote this book after my daughter left for college, as the beginning of the empty nest was upon me. If you experience a loss, and you will, you must strive to pick yourself up and move on. Otherwise, life will bring you and those around you down.

Whether you win or lose, prevail or fail, the key to success is what you learn from either the win or the loss and how you behave in doing so, which reminds me of what I love about a game. One of my favorite aspects of a sports game is when the whistle blows, and the athletes line up and high-five and hug one another. Good sportsmanship is key, whether you are the winner or you have suffered a loss. And in business or personally, people who want to spend time with you or hire or recruit you will quickly learn that you are either a good player, a good sport, a team player, a good person or not. When you are in the public eye, you are constantly being watched. So taking a win humbly and losing with grace is ever so important.

I find it interesting that wins and losses are not really so different. In both situations, you must review the game, your presentation, your speech, or your conversation to break down and discuss what worked and what might have been improved upon, adjusted, or changed. Clearly, you are in a different frame of mind whether you've won or lost, but what you do is the same.

Review what happened, reflect on it, and breathe in new life. The key to moving forward and learning from our past is through our wins and each loss, where we gain a new perspective.

Here are a few phrases to contemplate:

- Learn from what you did well, and break down what needs improvement
- Stillness, mindfulness, reflection
- Lessons occur in solitude
- Importance of being non-judgmental
- Give yourself the grace to be open-minded
- Feedback vs. criticism for a better outcome
- Learning from the lesson vs. beating yourself down
- There is no failure, only lessons learned

GOALS | Write It Out

Choose a conversation you recently participated in, a speech you delivered, or a presentation you made. Write out a plan for how you are going to do things differently when you have the next opportunity. How are you going to adjust and improve upon your approach?

____

____

ACTION | Move Forward

What could I have done differently? What could I have done better?

____

____

CONNECT | Who Can Help Me?

What do I need help with?

____

____

Chapter 15

Impact of The Mindset in Motion Method™

"Mindset creates the vision. Motion creates the impact."—Debbi DiMaggio

Shortly after someone gets to know me, they quickly learn through deeper conversations that whenever I set a goal, I conquer it. If I have something on my mind, it will fester until I do something about it. A lot of people set goals, yet they fail to follow through. My goal in writing this book is to inspire more people to take action. The importance of The Mindset In Motion Method™ is to find inspiration so that you, too, will act and move forward. By breaking down the steps and simplifying the process we make it possible. I began using this method long before the method was formally conceptualized. And in writing this book, I did not realize quite how much I utilized The Mindset In Motion until I broke down each goal I had achieved.

Activation Is Key

The diagram demonstrates your Wheel of Fortune.

There's a common misconception that in order to achieve your goal, you must do it alone. The Mindset In Motion Method will set you up for success because it encourages you to take action and to ask for support when you need it. Reach out to partners and peers, find an accountability partner, and join a networking or support group; the list is endless. There is a group for everything you can imagine, and most likely, your goal is something others have achieved before you. Even though it is your goal, you can still call in your wingmen, a support team, or even an army of professionals and experts to help you get dialed in for a win.

Messi, one of, if not THE best soccer players in the world, has a team of experts surrounding him. Noted is a list of those professionals:

- Fitness Coach
- Strength & Conditioning Coach
- Speed & Agility Coach
- Performance Coach
- Network Spinal Analysis (NSA) Chiropractor
- Acupuncturist
- Sports Scientist
- Sports Psychologist
- Physiotherapist
- Soft-Tissue/Massage Therapist
- Rehab Specialist
- Medical Doctor / Team Doctor
- Nutritionist
- Personal Trainer
- Recovery Specialist (cryotherapy, modalities, etc.)
- Personal Chef (performance-focused)
- Lifestyle/Routine Coach (informal but common)
- Emotional/Mental Health Therapist
- Mindset Coach
- Tactical Coach (club manager)
- Assistant Tactical Coach

- Position-Specific Coach (forward/attacking coach)
- Video Analyst
- Data Analyst
- Leadership Coach
- Video Coach

Overwhelming, right? The point is, you can find the right people to support you in whatever it is you want to do or goal or goals you desire to achieve.

As a member of the National Association of Divorce Professionals, I have come to learn that there are many experts who are available to help couples and families through this tumultuous time and process. As a real estate advisor, I am just one professional. The following is a list of many other experts: Divorce attorneys, family law attorneys, collaborative divorce attorneys, mediators, guardians ad litem, CPAs, forensic accountants, Certified Divorce Financial Analysts (CDFAs), business valuation experts, actuaries, financial planners, wealth advisors, therapists, licensed marriage and family therapists (LMFTs), divorce coaches, child therapists, child psychologists, co-parenting counselors, parenting coordinators, custody evaluators, child specialists, educational consultants, real estate divorce specialists, real estate appraisers, mortgage brokers, home organizers, home stagers, professional mediators, family facilitators, life coaches, transition coaches, spiritual counselors, pastoral counselors, estate planning attorneys, insurance advisors, career coaches, relocation specialists, concierge services, personal assistants, domestic-violence advocates, addiction counselors, immigration attorneys, special-needs consultants. The point I am trying to drive home, experts can help us achieve desired results.

Your Support System, the Universe

Imagine *you* as the sun, the radiant center of your life. Around you, your support system orbits like planets, each with its own gravity, energy, and role.

The Night the Sky Reminded Me of My Son

The morning my son left for OCS for Marine training, I was running in misty, heavy fog through the streets of Carmel, exhausted, emotional, and carrying the heavy quiet that settles in a mother's heart when her child leaves home to become someone stronger, braver, and more disciplined than you can even imagine. The house felt emptier without him. His presence, focused, determined, and full of momentum, had been a steady force in our home. And though I was so proud of him, I still felt the ache of change, of distance, of letting go. I wondered how he was sleeping, whether he was scared, and whether he felt alone.

One evening, as I breathed into the stillness, I looked up and saw the moon glowing brightly in a deep, expansive sky. Stars scattered like markers, each one shining in its own position, each one held by a gravitational order far greater than I could comprehend. And suddenly, he was there with me.

During boot camp, my son learned one of the most powerful truths of the Marine Corps: You may fight as an individual, but you stand because of your unit. He told me once, "Mom, you learn to be strong for yourself, but you survive because of your team." Staring at the moon that night, I realized I had my own version of that truth. I am the sun, the center of my own life, but I am not meant to shine alone. Just as my son relied on the structure, brotherhood, and discipline around him, I, too, had a universe orbiting around me:

- My husband, grounded and unwavering, my Earth.

- My daughter, creative and expressive, a planet of inspiration and emotion.

- My friends, dependable, energizing, and protective, like Jupiter.

- My mentors, colleagues, and clients, each offering clarity, accountability, and purpose.

- My wellness rituals, my emotional moon, pulling me back into alignment.

My son wasn't alone in his transformation. And neither was I. That night, the sky reminded me of something essential: you move forward not just because of your inner strength, but because of the universe of support that surrounds you. All you have to do is look up, acknowledge it, and allow yourself to be held.

The Universe Carries You Forward

Your support system is not a list of people. It is an energetic landscape, a solar system, orbiting your inner sun. When your sun shines bright, everything around you becomes stronger, steadier, and more aligned. When it dims, your system doesn't collapse. It simply waits for you to return to the center.

Whether you're building a business, navigating a transition, or stepping into a new chapter of identity, your support system becomes your gravitational field, the force that keeps you grounded, empowered, and in motion.

The Sun: Your Identity, Purpose & Inner Fire

You are the sun of your universe. Your sun is your:

- purpose
- clarity
- self-belief
- inner discipline
- willingness to act even when you're afraid

Marine training is built on discipline as a way of life, not just a skill. From day one, it teaches that discipline is doing the right thing, the right way, every time, especially when it's hard. Mindset in Motion teaches self-direction, the ability to lead your own life with strength, conviction, and intention.

Your light shines brightest when you know who you are and where you're headed."

The Moon: Emotional Gravity & Inner Guidance

Your moon represents the emotional landscape that shapes your daily experience:

- Self-care rituals
- Reflection and journaling
- Mindfulness and breathwork
- Honoring feelings instead of pushing past them
- Letting yourself pause

Your emotional world matters. It shapes your decisions, your energy, and the way you show up. Strengthening your moon creates balance, intuition, and resilience.

The Planets: The Support System Orbiting Your Life

Each planet in your universe offers a different kind of support:

Family: Unconditional love and grounding energy.

Friends: Truth-tellers, encouragers, and companions in both joy and transition.

Mentors & Coaches: Guides who elevate your mindset and hold you accountable.

Professional Team: The practical, operational, and creative support that helps you execute and expand.

Wellness: The people, practices, and routines that nourish your body, mind, and spirit.

Community: Clients, acquaintances, collaborators, neighbors, your extended circle of influence.

Some orbits are closer, some farther. Some shift as you evolve. All contribute to your strength.

Gravity, Energy, and Motion

Just like a solar system, your support system runs on balance. When you recognize the people and energies in your orbit, you move forward with more ease, confidence, and trust. When you neglect your system, or try to operate as if you are an entire universe on your own, you burn out. **The Mindset in Motion Method teaches this truth:**

"Momentum is never created in isolation. Momentum is created through rhythm, connection, and support."

Mindset in Motion Prompts

GOALS | Write It Out

1. Identify My Solar System. Write down the people, teams, and practices that support my life. Name my "planets," family, friends, mentors, wellness team.

____

____

2. Clarify My Sun. What purpose or dream is at the center of my current chapter?

____

____

3. Strengthen My Moon. Define 1–3 emotional wellness practices that keep me grounded.

____

____

4. Acknowledge My Marine-Level Resilience. What part of me has grown stronger through discipline or adversity?

____

____

ACTION | Move Forward

1. **Reach Out to One Planet Today.** Send a message, schedule a call, ask for support, or simply say thank you.

____

____

2. **Reinforce My Moon Ritual.** Do one practice today, journaling, walking, meditation, hydration, or breathwork.

____

____

3. **Refuel My Sun.** Take one step toward my central goal, even a small one.

____

____

4. **Shift One Orbit.** Are there people or energies I need to bring closer or move farther away?

____

____

CONNECT | Who Can Help Me?

1. **Share My Universe.** Tell someone close to me about the solar system metaphor. Notice how they respond.

---

2. Ask for Alignment. Invite a mentor, friend, or colleague to support my current goal or challenge.

Create a Shared Orbit. Identify one person I want to grow with in this chapter, a workout partner, accountability buddy, or creative collaborator.

---

3. Honor the Team That Moves With Me. Like the Marines, look around and acknowledge the people marching beside me.

Epilogue

Writing this book is one more example of the title that perfectly captures my life: *Accidentally with Purpose*. I was sharing that thought with a woman seated next to me on a flight. As I told her my story and repeated the phrase, she paused and asked, "Was it really by accident?" That question stayed with me. Did I create every opening? Every opportunity?

Before I started this book, or even had the idea, I set out to take a course to prepare me for a TEDx Talk. When I discovered a TEDx course on Instagram, I purchased it and immediately went into motion, diving into the material with excitement and zeal.

As I began combing through the course, answering each question, elaborating, and moving into the next, I stopped to ask myself, "What would be that ideal topic?" As I wrote out my thoughts and ideas, I realized I had too much material and too many different subjects to speak on. I became overwhelmed. I did, however, continue to write in order to get my thoughts down on paper.

Early the next morning it dawned on me that I had to write another book. I had to find clarity. For one, I had to hone my message down so finely that I could speak comfortably for 15 minutes without losing my train of thought. It's how I do everything in life. I must have a full understanding of whatever it is so I am confident to execute. I continued to fill my notes on three topics -Real

Estate, the Empty Nest, and Goal Setting. Goal Setting included specifics on how I had achieved my goals so I could teach others to do the same.

Time passed, and I dropped the TEDx Talk idea as I launched into writing book number 6. Fast forward, when I got to a point where I thought I was finished with the mini pocketbook, I had begun reaching out to book editors and other book experts. Fully in motion and on a mission, I spoke with two wonderful people on the East Coast who were kind, insightful, and generous with their guidance.

The next day, as life so often does, surprised me. I attended a women's networking meeting, something I do regularly, as I'm always looking to expand my real estate network, and that's when and where it happened. In Beverly Hills, at a meeting I decided to attend just the day before. And that is where I met Ellie - accidentally *with purpose*. The moment we spoke, I knew she was the one.

When I started working with Ellie, she said to me, "You have 3 books in you; where do you want to start?" Where I started is not where I ended up. When I started the process, I visualized myself in a room full of people giving my TEDx Talk, I could imagine the blank stares; even if an audience is supportive, they can still give off a look of boredom. As it were, I bypassed the TEDx course and moved on to write this book. While writing this book, I have gained such clarity that my message seemingly flows out and onto the pages, the sort of flow I intended and intend to have one day when I do give my TEDx Talk.

During this journey, I've shared *The Mindset in Motion Method* in front of our real estate partner company in New York, on my own podcast, *Mastering the Art of Success*, and as a guest on several other podcasts. My message began to flow, blossoming within me. It has become everything I hoped it would be. I feel intimately connected to my content, as though it has taken root inside me and is now carrying me forward.

My next big step will be speaking on stage. It's something I've always envisioned, but until now, I hadn't felt it in my gut. Today, it's becoming more familiar, just as real estate has been for over 35 years. The information, the structure, the message… It's crystal clear. And it is my greatest desire to share my story with you, to inspire you to follow your passion, live your purpose, conquer your goals, and step boldly into your next chapter.

Just as I was headed one way, I pivoted and found myself on a different path. Once you're in motion, momentum has a way of taking you somewhere new, and that's okay. When you choose something, don't allow yourself to feel overwhelmed. Simply pick up and begin. With each step, it will start to grow arms, legs, and even tentacles or branches. Eventually, it will take root like a tree, unexpectedly, or *accidentally with purpose*.

Your Final Personal Audit

What Are My Goals in Each Category

Personal Relationship

____

____

Professional

____

____

Hobbies

____

____

Health + Fitness

____

____

MY BIG GOAL | My Life's Mission

____

____

If you would like to book a consultation with me to review your goals, reach out. DebbiDiMaggio.com

About the Author

Debbi DiMaggio is a real estate advisor, author, speaker, and entrepreneur known for turning vision into results. As a top-producing Realtor with Corcoran Icon Properties and co-founder of The DiMaggio Betta Group, she has built a respected, relationship-driven business rooted in strategy, discipline, and long-term trust, guiding clients through complex real estate decisions across all stages of life.

She is also the Founder of *Foundation For Success*, a five-step framework and business system designed for entrepreneurs, brands, and service professionals ready to elevate and scale. Built on the belief that just as every home needs a strong foundation, so does every successful business, her methodology provides the structure, clarity, and momentum needed for long-term growth. Her signature *5 C's of Real Estate*—principles proven in the field—also translate seamlessly into broader business success.

Beyond real estate, Debbi is the creator of *The Mindset In Motion Method*™, a five-step performance framework:

Goal. Believe. Internalize. Share. Activate.

Designed to help professionals and entrepreneurs bridge inspiration with decisive action, her work centers on mindset, accountability, and aligned execution as the foundation for sustainable success.

She is the host of the podcast *Mastering the Art of Success* (formerly *Mastering the Art of Real Estate*), where she interviews leaders, designers, and entrepreneurs who exemplify excellence in business and life.

Through writing, speaking, and brand building, Debbi challenges individuals to think expansively, move intentionally, and create results that reflect their highest potential.

Her philosophy: Mindset. Movement. Results.

Reflection: Tuning the Signal

In 2017, before Los Angeles was part of my everyday rhythm, I found myself lying on a chiropractic table in a softly lit room alongside four to eight other people, surrendering to something I didn't fully understand. Dr. Liz Dobbins practiced Network Spinal Analysis. She would move quietly from one person to the next, barely touching our backs, her hands resting lightly along the spine as if listening to something beneath the surface. Around me, emotions surfaced without warning. One woman cried. Another screamed. The air felt charged, almost sacred. When my daughter Bianca came with me once, she couldn't believe what she was witnessing. Neither could I, if I'm honest.

I didn't have language for what was happening in my body. At times tears slipped out, but never violently. Mostly there was a subtle unwinding — sensations rising and falling, like something long-held beginning to loosen. I often left not knowing exactly what I had felt, only that something had shifted. And so I kept going back. I have always believed in experiencing life fully, even when I cannot yet explain it.

Nearly eight years later, as I was writing the final pages of this book, I reached out to Dr. Liz and asked her what had truly been happening during those sessions. She explained that stress and trauma create distortions in the nervous system, locking us into patterns of fight or flight and limiting our self-expression. Parts of the self — parts of the soul — get placed quietly on a shelf when survival takes over. Network care works through the body to release those distortions, to restore coherence, to strengthen what she called our authentic signal — our soul signature.

And suddenly it became clear. The work I was doing back then was not random. It was not simply curiosity. It was preparation. It was what expanded my capacity to finally live between my home in Northern California and a second home in Los Angeles. Before I could stretch my life geographically, I had to stretch neurologically. My nervous system had to feel safe enough to expand. The move was not just about opportunity or ambition. It was about alignment. My body had to believe it was possible before my life could follow.

Create Your Mindset in Motion Blueprint

Now that you have completed the tables for each step: Goal, Believe, Internalize, Share, and Activate — it's time to bring everything together. This is where clarity becomes structure. Review your responses from each section. Look for patterns. Notice repeated words, emotional themes, fears you identified, strengths you claimed, and actions you committed to. Then, synthesize your answers into one cohesive blueprint, a clear, written roadmap that captures:

- The goal you are committed to
- The belief you are choosing to strengthen
- The identity you are stepping into
- The support and accountability you will lean on
- The specific actions you will take

Your Blueprint should not be a list. It should be read as a declaration, a concise, integrated plan that reflects who you are becoming and how you will move forward. Think of it as your personal operating system. A document you can return to when doubt surfaces. A reminder of the alignment between your mindset, your nervous system, and your actions.

Below is my example of a Mindset in Motion Blueprint so you can see how the pieces come together.

Mindset in Motion Method™ Blueprint

Goal and Vision: Retire at 65 and maintain my current lifestyle without cutting back on expenses

1. GOAL

My goal is clear and non-negotiable: I am retiring at age 65 while continuing to live the lifestyle I enjoy today, my home, travel, experiences, generosity, and everyday comforts — all fully supported by the income and assets I've built. This is not about "getting by." This is about freedom, choice, and security.

2. BELIEVE

I truly believe this is possible for me. I believe:

- I am capable of making smart financial decisions
- There is still plenty of time to grow and prepare
- Money can work for me when I'm intentional
- My future self is worth planning for

I am not behind. I am right on time. Every step I take now compounds in my favor.

3. INTERNALIZE

I am training my mind to see this retirement as my reality, not just a wish.

Here's how I make this part of who I am:

- I have written my retirement vision in detail

- I read it regularly and picture my life at 65, calm, secure, and enjoying the same lifestyle I love now

- I meditate on this future, feeling the peace and confidence of being financially prepared

- My written goal is posted on my mirror so I see it every day

- I bought a journal dedicated to this chapter of life

- I write in it daily, affirming, refining, and expanding my vision

- I created a vision board and a Pinterest board filled with images of the life I'm designing

This is no longer "someday." This is the life I am actively building.

4. SHARE

I don't carry this vision alone. I share it with people who support my growth and future. I talk about my retirement goals with:

- Trusted friends

- Supportive family members

- Mentors and financially savvy people in my circle

Speaking it out loud makes it more real. The right people encourage me, hold me accountable, and sometimes introduce me to opportunities I wouldn't find on my own.

5. ACTIVATE

Belief without action is just a dream, so I move.

Here's how I am actively turning my vision into reality:

- I am meeting with three financial planners to understand my options and create a clear retirement strategy

- I am joining a community where people talk openly about money, growth, and future planning

- I am taking classes to increase my financial knowledge and confidence

- I am committed to saving consistently

- I am investing intentionally for long-term growth

- I am regularly putting money away specifically for retirement

Every dollar I save and invest is a vote for my future freedom. (Speak in the affirmative)

My Identity Moving Forward

- I am a woman who plans wisely.

- I am someone who prepares for the future with clarity and confidence.

- I am building a retirement that supports the life I love — not one that limits it.

- I am in motion. And my future self is already thanking me.

Producing a Film Using the Mindset In Motion Method™

Mindset. Movement. Results.

Producing a film is not just a creative endeavor, it's a leadership test. It requires clarity, conviction, collaboration, and disciplined execution. The Mindset In Motion Method™ provides a structured way to move a film from concept to completion.

I. GOAL

Every successful production begins with a clearly defined goal. What story are you telling? Why does it matter? Who is it for? Without clarity at the beginning, momentum fades in the middle. A producer must define the vision and desired outcome before inviting others into the journey.

2. BELIEVE

Belief is the producer's most valuable asset. Independent film, especially, is filled with uncertainty, funding gaps, scheduling challenges, creative pivots. The producer must believe in the script, the director, the cast, and the long-term impact of the story before others will. Belief builds confidence. Confidence attracts support.

3. INTERNALIZE

Producing is not passive investment, its ownership. To internalize a project means fully understanding:

- The creative direction
- The budget and financial structure
- The risk and reward
- The timeline and production demands

When you internalize the mission, you move from observer to leader.

4. SHARE

Films are collaborative ecosystems. A producer must communicate the vision clearly to:

- Investors
- Creative partners
- Cast and crew
- Distributors and festival networks

Sharing is strategic. It's not just about promotion, it's about alignment. The right people rally around a clearly articulated vision.

5. ACTIVATE

Ideas don't make films. Action does. Activation includes:

- Securing financing
- Structuring agreements

- Managing logistics
- Keeping the team accountable
- Driving the project across the finish line

This is where mindset turns into movement, and movement turns into measurable results.

THE RESULT

When the Mindset In Motion Method™ is applied to film production, the outcome is more than a completed movie. It builds:

- Leadership credibility
- Strategic partnerships
- Industry relationships
- Brand authority
- Long-term opportunity

Producing a film is not just a creative act. It is a disciplined business decision powered by an aligned mindset and sustained action.

From Realtor to Executive Producer: A Mindset In Motion™ Story

Mindset. Movement. Results.

James Morosini reached out to me on Twitter. I responded. That small decision, to engage instead of scroll past, was the spark. At the time, I was a Realtor, not a film producer. When James and Sam Sonenshine explained that producing required the same core skills I already used in business, relationship building, raising capital, generating interest, I paused.

Then I leaned in. Nothing ventured, nothing gained. I agreed to meet James and Sam in Beverly Hills to hear their pitch. I went as a listener. I was curious. They reminded me of my son and his friend, ambitious, creative, and driven. I saw belief in them before the outcome existed. That belief moved me. It was an emotional time in my life.

GOAL

The goal became clear: help bring this film to life. Not because I had film credits. But because I understood how to rally support around a vision.

BELIEVE

When they explained that my role would focus on raising awareness, attracting funding, and building interest, something clicked. I already had those skills. Producing wasn't about the title. It was about execution. So I believed in them and in my ability to contribute.

INTERNALIZE

At some point, it stopped being "their film." It became our film. I committed fully. I didn't stand on the sidelines questioning whether I belonged in the room. I stepped into responsibility.

SHARE

I launched a GoFundMe campaign. I reached out to my network. I asked. Asking requires courage. But I moved anyway. And then something powerful happened, my friend Debi made a generous contribution. That single act created momentum. It validated the risk and energized the effort.

ACTIVATE

I didn't wait to feel qualified. I didn't overthink the opportunity. I acted. And through that action, I stepped into the role of **Executive Producer**. Before writing these 2 words, Executive Producer, I double checked IMDb to confirm it was still real after 9 years. And it was. Oftentimes I feel it was just a dream. 2018 was a pivotal moment and year in my life. I went on to produce Break Cute helping out yet another young entrepreneur and childhood friend of my daughter.

Selection and the Moment That Changed Everything

The film was selected to screen at the **Silicon Valley Film Festival**. We attended the festival together. I sat in the theater watching a project that began as a Twitter message evolved into a fully realized film on screen. The lights dimmed. The credits began to roll. And then I saw my name:

Executive Producer, Debbi DiMaggio or was it

Debbi DiMaggio, Executive Producer

At that moment I felt Pride, Shock, and Overwhelm - because I did it. Not because I was ready, But because I responded. I believed. I activated.

The Ripple Effect

After that experience, other producers reached out and asked me to help with additional projects. Because once you demonstrate that you can move vision into reality, doors open. And more importantly, your own self-belief expands.

The Leadership Lesson

Mindset In Motion™ isn't theory.

It's the courage to say yes before you feel ready.

It's trusting that your skills transfer.

It's taking action when others hesitate.

You don't wait to be chosen.

You move.

And sometimes, that movement leads to your name scrolling across a screen in a darkened theater, proof that leadership belongs to those who activate.

Mindset. Movement. Results.

	PERSONAL GOAL
GOAL	
BELIEVE	
INTERNALIZE	
SHARE	
ACTIVATE	

	PROFESSIONAL GOAL
GOAL	328
BELIEVE	
INTERNALIZE	
SHARE	
ACTIVATE	

	FINANCIAL GOAL
GOAL	
BELIEVE	
INTERNALIZE	
SHARE	
ACTIVATE	

	HEALTH & WELLNESS GOAL
GOAL	
BELIEVE	
INTERNALIZE	
SHARE	
ACTIVATE	

	SPIRITUAL GOAL
GOAL	
BELIEVE	
INTERNALIZE	
SHARE	
ACTIVATE	

Follow @DebbiDiMaggio to access your Mindset In Motion™ 90-Day Momentum Planner—created for leaders ready to activate.

Words To Live By

A few more favorite quotes I uncovered during the year I spent working on this book. Add your own as your next chapter unfolds.

"It's not who you are that holds you back; it's who you think you're not." – Unknown

"Every accomplishment starts with the decision to try." – Gail Devers

"Setbacks will come. Stay resilient. Your voice is the only one that matters."

"Discipline sets your boundaries. Structure shows you the way. Without them, your goals are just wishes."

"Morning routines ground you. Rituals prepare you. Together, they set the tone for everything that follows."

"Being coachable doesn't make you weak—it makes you unstoppable. The more you learn, the faster you grow."

"No excuses. No is not an option. There's always a way—move forward and find it."

"David never called it suffering. His mindset was bigger than the pain. His story reminds me: if he could push through that, I can conquer anything."

"His story taught me this: when your goals are bigger than your pain, nothing can stop you."

"We become what we think about." — Earl Nightingale

"Failure is simply the opportunity to begin again, this time more intelligently." - Henry Ford.

"I have not failed. I've just found 10,000 ways that won't work." - Thomas Edison

"Whether you think you can, or you think you can't—you're right." — Henry Ford

"The mind is everything. What you think, you become." — Buddha

"Your life does not get better by chance; it gets better by change." — Jim Rohn

"Mindset combined with preparation creates results." Debbi DiMaggio

"To be a champ, you have to believe in yourself when no one else will." — Sugar Ray Robinson

"What the mind can conceive and believe, it can achieve." — Napoleon Hill

"A lead is only as safe as the time remaining allows."

"Until the clock hits zero, the game isn't over."

"The greatest comeback isn't in the scoreboard — it's in the belief that you can change the result in the final moments."

"Late lead changes are a reminder that momentum shifts can happen at any time — even when you're ahead."

"Even when you believe victory is assured, the final seconds demand every ounce of focus."

And so it is. —Alexis Summerfield

The Spark

That ignited the flame. The catalyst that created movement. The moment belief turned into action.

The Catalyst

Matt Murray. Inspired by his teacher, to pursue his acting dream.

A Quote

On social media, sparked my response, led to an email, and became the beginning of a friendship with Bob Burg, once a stranger.

A Song

A reminder that my story wasn't finished, there were still I chapters waiting to be written.

A Question

"How about the Piedmont office?" A simple suggestion posed by Heidi, sparked the launch of Highland Partners.

An Idea

What began as a TEDx course evolved into this book.

A Conversation

One moment. One exchange. That shifted your perspective and changed your direction.

A Challenge

A moment of doubt that became the very reason you moved forward.

A Setback

What felt like an ending became the beginning of something greater.

A Mentor

A few words, spoken at the right time that changed everything.

A Blank Page

An invitation to begin before you felt ready.

A Feeling

A quiet knowing that there was more, and it was time to act.

A Missed Opportunity

The one you couldn't stop thinking about, that whispered, next time, say yes.

A Chance Encounter

A stranger. A few words. And suddenly, a new path appeared.

A Late Night

When you couldn't sleep because the idea wouldn't let you go.

A Door That Closed

What felt like rejection redirected you to where you were meant to be.

A Risk

The moment you said yes before you had it all figured out.

A Nudge

That quiet voice that wouldn't go away, until you listened.

A First Step

Small. Uncertain. Imperfect. But it changed everything.

A Failure

The lesson that reshaped your direction and strengthened your resolve.

A Win

Proof that you were capable of more than you imagined.

A Season of Waiting

When nothing seemed to be happening, everything was forming.

A Pivot

When you realized you didn't have to stay where you started.

A Commitment

The moment you decided: no more waiting.

The Spark

Looks different for everyone. But it's always there, waiting to be recognized, waiting to be acted on. Every movement begins with a spark. What was yours?

www.ingramcontent.com/pod-product-compliance
Lightning Source LLC
Chambersburg PA
CBHW051500150726
47997CB00001B/55